HALF BAKED HARVEST

super simple

HALF BAKED HARVEST

super simple

MORE THAN 125 RECIPES for INSTANT, OVERNIGHT,
MEAL-PREPPED, and EASY COMFORT FOODS

TIEGHAN GERARD

CLARKSON POTTER/PUBLISHERS
NEW YORK

To my supportive *Half Baked Harvest* family, this book is dedicated to you! Without you and your requests for a second book, this cookbook certainly would not be. Thank you for continuing to read each day, to re-create recipes, and to share them through Instagram, emails, and comments. Thank you for your feedback—without it, I may never have got ten to super simple.

CONTENTS

INTRODUCTION

I COME FROM A FAMILY OF NINE—and a big family means big meals. In an effort to control some of our mealtime chaos and get dinner on the table before ten p.m., when I was thirteen years old, I began to help my dad with the cooking. Within a few months, I was cooking dinner for the entire family every single night—I loved it immediately. I have always been a creative person, so I started expressing my artistic side through cooking. I had fun dreaming up my own recipes, experimenting with new types of cuisines and ingredients, and putting my own twist on classics. At nineteen, I decided to capture the process in photographs and began to document my favorite recipes on *Half Baked Harvest*. I had no idea what I was doing at the time, but fast-forward several years and *Half Baked Harvest* has become a full-time career that keeps me *extremely* busy. In fact, my mom, my dad, and one of my brothers work for the company!

When I first started out, I was young, still living in my parents' house, and I had all the time in the world to spend in the kitchen creating elaborate recipes. But I've had to adapt to a much busier lifestyle. My life now encompasses so much more than recipe development and photography. There's travel, management of my team, and the demands of trying to grow the business. Like most everyone else in the world, I need simple, quick, everyday recipes that come together in a flash but still taste delicious. As my own cooking began to veer more into the territory of simplicity, I began sharing them and—surprise, surprise—they quickly became pretty darn popular.

I'm willing to bet you're just as busy as I am, if not more so. The first thing to go when life gets hectic is meal planning and cooking, right? You get home at the end of the day, you didn't plan ahead, you don't have what you need, and you're too tired to think. Well, I'm going to help you with all of that. In fact, this idea was born solely from the feedback I received from you guys. Your emails, Instagram messages, and comments on *Half Baked Harvest* said it loud and clear: more recipes that are delicious but EASY, too. This book is exactly that: my go-to super simple recipes. My purpose in creating *Half Baked Harvest* has always been to help readers get into the kitchen and create tasty, healthy(ish) recipes any day of the week. This cookbook is another tool for you to do just that.

ABOUT THIS BOOK

HERE'S WHAT YOU NEED TO KNOW: Within this cookbook I'm sharing some of my favorite recipes. They are flavorful, colorful, and easy. Some of them are healthy . . . and some have a good amount of cheese. It's all about balance.

Just because these recipes are super simple does not mean they lack flavor. While these recipes are straightforward enough for everyday cooking, they do not fall exclusively into the ten-ingredients-or-fewer and made-in-under-thirty-minutes categories—though there *are* plenty of both! Flavor has always been and will always be paramount to me. Of course, I want to share the easiest version of a recipe, but I will not sacrifice taste to make a dish with only five ingredients. That said, some of the recipes included here have more than ten ingredients and some take longer than thirty minutes, but that doesn't mean the recipe is not "super simple." If you can throw ingredients into a slow cooker, use an Instant Pot, dump them all in one skillet, or simply pick up a few items from the grocery store to assemble something quick, you can handle these recipes. You'll definitely be adding these recipes to your weeknight lineup.

You can, of course, still expect all my special "Tieghan touches," which can range from including an unexpected ingredient or garnishing with herbs or edible flowers. I'm still me—I'm just shorter on time! The extra flourishes not working for you? Skip 'em! Really, you have my permission. Making recipes beautiful and pleasing to the eye is what I'm all about—it's a priority for me—but, please, take or leave these "extras" as you wish! (I will say, though, if you are looking to up your Instagram game, an edible flower or two is always a good start.)

I've organized the book by types of meals and popular main ingredients: breakfast, appetizers and sides, salad and soup, pizza and pasta, vegetarian, poultry and pork, meat, seafood, and last (but certainly not least, not here!) dessert. So, all your basic and most loved food groups, right? I have also included a chapter on my favorite super simple basic recipes because homemade still tastes better—and making meals from scratch doesn't have to be difficult or a time suck. On these pages, you'll find slow cooker dinners, Instant Pot recipes, one pan goodness, recipes made with exclusively pantry staple ingredients, recipes with fewer than ten ingredients (not including salt, pepper, or olive oil), recipes that take thirty minutes or less, and some of my best tips and tricks for easy cooking. Whenever possible, I have given slow cooker, pressure cooker, *and* stovetop options to make the recipes completely adaptable for your needs. Look for the icons at the right throughout the recipe pages.

There is something for everyone here . . . and a photo to go along with it, too.

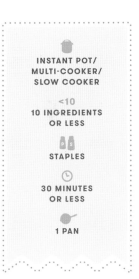

**INSTANT POT/
MULTI-COOKER/
SLOW COOKER**

<10
**10 INGREDIENTS
OR LESS**

STAPLES

**30 MINUTES
OR LESS**

1 PAN

STOCK UP AND SET UP FOR SUCCESS

Step one to "super simple" cooking is to keep a well-stocked pantry. It's something my mom taught me years ago when we'd bake chocolate chip cookies together after school. Of course, my mom's pantry was mostly full of Nestlé Toll House Chocolate Morsels and pasta . . . she obviously had her priorities straight.

Some of my favorite meals are composed of pantry staples, so, naturally, my pantry is stocked with the items I use most often: lots of Asian sauces, spices, canned tomatoes, nuts, seeds, anything that I can use to quickly throw together a delicious meal in minutes. It's important to have the ingredients that you use most often always on hand. When your pantry is stocked, you can make an incredible soup (see my Butter-Roasted Tomato Soup with Honey'd Brie Grilled Cheese, page 103), a quick salad (like my Everything Bagel Salad with White Beans and Pesto, page 80), cheesy pizza (you must make my Potato and Burrata Pizza, page 117), and even a good cookie bar for dessert (the Chocolate Peanut Butter Blondie Brownie Bars on page 274 are life

changing) without stressing or having to make a run to the store.

When it comes to grocery shopping, I never go without a list. My best tip? Use the notes app on your phone (Isn't your phone your number one accessory?) to keep a running list of the things you need to keep your pantry fully loaded. You'll always know exactly what you need when you pop into the store after work—no lost or forgotten slips of paper.

Meal planning takes a bit more organization, but it's completely worth the effort. Set aside some time on Saturday or Sunday morning to map out your meals for the week before hitting the grocery store. I like to get this out of the way first thing in the morning before the crowds surge later in the afternoon. Then spend a couple of hours on Sunday prepping food and doing any cooking you can before your busy workweek starts. Once you get into the habit, putting dinner on the table every night of the week is a piece of cake. (And, yes, I recommend making sure you have a piece of cake each night, too!)

FOR THE PANTRY

There is no reason not to have a stocked pantry. Most shelf-stable items will last for months, some even years, before expiring. With these ingredients at the ready, you will be able to create balanced and delicious meals even when your fridge is looking sad and empty.

DRY GOODS

BAKING POWDER AND BAKING SODA Essential. Just make sure each is fresh before using. In general, each will last six to twelve months, but most bakers recommend replacing every six months to ensure freshness.

BEANS AND LENTILS Legumes are a healthy source of protein to add to almost anything that needs to be a little heartier.

BREAD CRUMBS A must-have for breading chicken or topping soup. I like to use panko if I'm not making my own.

CHOCOLATE (DARK, SEMISWEET, AND MILK) Possibly the most important pantry staple? My mom thinks so.

COCONUT, FLAKED Unsweetened and sweetened are delicious in bread and muffins.

CRACKERS, ASSORTED For an impromptu cheese board.

FLOURS all-purpose, white, whole-wheat, gluten-free blend. For baking and cooking.

GRAINS basmati rice, wild rice, quinoa, polenta. Great for serving with things like chicken or stirring into soups, and even tossing with greens to make a hearty salad.

SPICES paprika, cumin, turmeric, chili powder, dried herbs. Spices are the key to a flavorful dish. Always keep your most-used on hand . . . and, for some, you might even want to have backups.

NUTS AND SEEDS raw cashews, almonds, pine nuts, pecans, peanuts, pepitas (pumpkin seeds), sunflower seeds. Perfect for snacking, tossing into salads, or topping off dishes for a nice crunch.

PASTA AND NOODLES spaghetti, penne, tagliatelle, rigatoni, bucatini, orzo, rice noodles, ramen. Keep all of your favorites on hand! There is no better pantry meal than a pasta dish.

SUGARS granulated and brown (light and dark), and confectioners'. Cookies, cakes, and all the sweets, please.

SHELF-STABLE LIQUIDS

BROTH chicken, veggie, and beef. Essential to creating soups, chilis, and sauces. I like to use low-sodium so I can better control the saltiness of my dish.

COCONUT MILK I always use full-fat canned coconut milk for best flavor and creaminess. All the recipes in this book call for full-fat. Be sure to give it a good shake before you open the can.

HONEY My go-to sweetener for both sweet and savory recipes.

HOT SAUCES I love Frank's RedHot and pretty much all the Tabasco flavors.

PURE MAPLE SYRUP Because no stack of pancakes is complete without the real stuff—I always buy pure.

OILS extra-virgin olive oil, sesame oil, toasted sesame oil, canola oil, and peanut oil. These oils are staples in pretty much every recipe.

VINEGARS apple cider, rice, champagne, red wine, and balsamic. Best for making tangy sauces and vinaigrettes.

MOLASSES Because you just never know when you'll need to bake gingerbread cookies.

SAUCES

ENCHILADA SAUCE Use for quick skillet enchiladas or a spicy pasta dish. There are so many ways to use enchilada sauce. Get creative.

FISH SAUCE One of my favorite ingredients and the key to cooking great Thai-inspired food.

SWEET THAI CHILI SAUCE Pour this over chicken and roast in the oven for a sticky, sweet, and spicy dinner with rice.

LOW-SODIUM SOY SAUCE OR TAMARI A great way to add a touch of salty flavor to almost any dish, Asian-inspired or not.

PURE VANILLA EXTRACT Should be used in most baked goods . . . whether the recipe calls for it or not.

CANNED AND JARRED CONDIMENTS, ETC.

BASIL PESTO It's my favorite ingredient to toss into pretty much any recipe to add not only flavor but also a vibrant swish of color.

MUSTARD Dijon or grainy: Add to a delicious creamy sauce or flavorful vinaigrette.

SAMBAL OELEK (CHILI PASTE) The perfect kick of heat. Great in pretty much any sauce.

THAI RED CURRY PASTE Add a can of coconut milk, some veggies, and you have the easiest curry on earth.

JAMS AND PRESERVES Add them to cocktails, use to spread over toast, make a damn good PB&J . . . or a savory-sweet grilled cheese. You can do so much with a dollop of good jam. I recommend stocking assorted flavors.

NUT BUTTERS For everything from snacking to baking. Tip? A square of dark chocolate, plus a bite of banana and a spoonful of peanut butter, makes the best midnight snack.

OLIVES Keep a mix of green and kalamata in the pantry for Mediterranean-inspired dishes or just to pair with cheese and meats for a quickie appetizer.

CHIPOTLE PEPPERS IN ADOBO Smoky and spicy, these are my favorite way to add a kick to any dish.

ROASTED RED PEPPERS Use these when your fridge has zero fresh vegetables. They are great pureed into sauces and tossed into pasta, and are delicious on sandwiches.

PICKLES Because when the craving strikes, you want to make sure you have pickles. Also? The little ones—cornichons? Those are essential on a meat and cheese board.

TOMATOES fire-roasted, crushed, whole, sun-dried (be sure to save the olive oil and use for sauces and vinaigrettes), tomato paste. An assortment of tomato products at the ready will inspire your cooking.

TUNA For the quickest protein-packed lunch, mix tuna (I like oil-packed) with avocado, soft-boiled eggs, herbs, lemon, and a pinch of flaky sea salt. Serve on toast.

LOOSE VEGETABLES

GARLIC, SHALLOTS, AND ONIONS I always have these essentials on hand, especially since they last way longer than you think (usually anywhere from 1 to 3 months when kept in a cool, dry place).

POTATOES AND WINTER SQUASH Great for roasting alongside meats and seafood . . . and, really, who doesn't love roasted potatoes? Best side dish for pretty much anything.

IN THE FRIDGE

Though the refrigerator might not be considered "the pantry," there are many staples you can stock up on weekly or even monthly.

DAIRY

SALTED BUTTER Always, always.

CHEESES, ASSORTED Hard cheeses like Parmesan can last weeks in the fridge. Be sure to save the rinds for a flavorful sauce or soup. I always have Parmesan, feta, cheddar, cream cheese, mascarpone, and ricotta.

EGGS Eggs keep longer than you think, 4 to 5 weeks. All the recipes in the book call for large eggs.

PLAIN GREEK YOGURT A staple for easy breakfasts and healthier sauces. All the recipes in this book call for full-fat.

FRESH HERBS Basil, cilantro, parsley, and thyme. These are always in the fridge to keep meals fresh and flavorful.

VEGETABLES AND MEAT

AVOCADO Once they are ripe, I stick avocados into the fridge to finish out their shelf life. They'll stay good for 1 to 2 weeks there.

CARROTS Carrots last forever . . . well, maybe not forever but for a while, and they're delish in salads, sauces, and soups.

FRESH GINGER I use ginger every day for extra-flavorful recipes with a little kick. Try my Gingered Thai Steak and Pepper Salad (page 87).

FRESH GREENS I keep spinach, arugula, or Tuscan kale on hand for a quick salad.

LEMONS/LIMES They're the key to a good salad dressing, can save just about any recipe from being bland, and are great in drinks and sparkling water.

PROSCIUTTO In case you need to make an impromptu cheese board, which, duh.

FOR THE FREEZER

Keeping a stocked freezer is just as important as keeping a stocked pantry. Freezer items can last for months, which comes in handy if you need to go into hibernation—or great when you're less busy and have time to cook, store, and freeze meals for your future busy self.

VEGETABLES

SPINACH AND BROCCOLI Frozen vegetables are a great option when you don't have fresh on hand.

MEAT AND SEAFOOD

GROUND CHICKEN/BEEF Pull out of the freezer the night before you need it, or in the morning for an easy dinner that night.

CHICKEN BREASTS OR THIGHS Pro tip—no need to thaw if using an Instant Pot. Just add an additional 3 to 5 minutes of cooking time to make up for the breasts being frozen.

SHRIMP/SEAFOOD All seafood thaws extremely quickly. Having it on hand in the freezer is great for busy nights and for weeks when you can't make it to the grocery store.

MISCELLANEOUS MUST-HAVES

BREAD For morning toast, soups, and homemade bread crumbs.

FROZEN FRUIT To make quick smoothies or even to bake with.

ICE CREAM If for no other reason than that after-party craving.

PUFF PASTRY One of my favorite things to have in the freezer at all times. Makes the perfect cheesy tart and so many other delicious, quick meals.

With that, pull up a chair, grab your pencil, calendar, laptop, maybe something to snack on, and start flipping through these recipes. Plan your meals, make a grocery list, stock your pantry, and then make your way into the kitchen to cook up a whole lot of goodness. Once you're finished, do as I would: take a photo, share it on Instagram (tag me @halfbakedharvest), and show everyone what you've made. I cannot wait to see all your delicious creations!

THE BASICS

EVERYDAY BREAD DOUGH

SERVES: 8

PREP TIME: 10 minutes
RESTING TIME: 1 hour
TOTAL TIME: 1 hour 10 minutes

This bread dough is going to save your life. I use it as a base for many recipes, both sweet and savory. It's soft, fluffy, and just a little bit buttery. The best part? The recipe is beyond simple. I may even go so far as to call it foolproof. Instant yeast is my secret weapon, as it eliminates an extra hour or two from the rising time. You'll see this dough pop up multiple times throughout the chapters of this book, but mostly in the breakfast chapter. Undeniably, I love a sweet pastry breakfast—my overnight cinnamon roll bread (see page 44) is a perennial favorite. You can store the dough, wrapped in plastic wrap, in the fridge for up to 3 days or in the freezer for up to 3 months. Just thaw the frozen dough overnight in the fridge and use as directed.

~ BASIC ~

1 cup warm whole milk

1 packet instant dry yeast

1 tablespoon honey

2 large eggs, beaten

4 tablespoons salted butter, melted

3½ to 4 cups all-purpose flour (see Note)

½ teaspoon kosher salt

1. In the bowl of a stand mixer fitted with the dough hook attachment, combine the milk, yeast, honey, eggs, butter, 3½ cups of flour, and the salt. Beat until the flour is completely incorporated, 4 to 5 minutes. If the dough seems sticky, add the remaining ½ cup of flour.

2. Cover the bowl with plastic wrap and let sit at room temperature until doubled in size, about 1 hour.

3. At this point, the dough can be used as directed within any recipe of your choice.

~ WHOLE-WHEAT ~

1 cup warm whole milk

1 packet instant dry yeast

1 tablespoon honey

2 large eggs, beaten

4 tablespoons salted butter, melted

1½ cups white flour, plus more as needed

2 cups whole-wheat pastry flour

½ teaspoon kosher salt

1. In the bowl of a stand mixer fitted with the dough hook attachment, combine the milk, yeast, honey, eggs, butter, both flours, and salt. Beat until the flour is completely incorporated, 4 to 5 minutes. If the dough seems sticky, add more white flour 1 tablespoon at a time.

2. Cover the bowl with plastic wrap and let sit at room temperature until doubled in size, about 1 hour.

3. At this point, the dough can be used as directed within any recipe of your choice.

To measure flour properly, fluff the flour in its bag or container with your measuring cup and sprinkle it into a dry bowl. Then scoop the flour back up with the measuring cup and level off the excess with a straightedge.

EVERYDAY PANCAKE MIX

MAKES: ABOUT 7 CUPS PANCAKE MIX

PREP TIME: 10 minutes
TOTAL TIME: 10 minutes

In our house, pancakes are one of our most loved breakfast foods. We make them all the time, and it's so nice to have the dry mix already combined and ready to go on a sleepy Sunday morning. I promise you, it's better than the boxed stuff. Just add a little melted butter, a splash of milk, some eggs, and maybe a touch of vanilla, and you'll have a yummy batter in five minutes. It's the base for the pumpkin butter pancakes (see page 35). You can use it for waffles, too!

4 cups whole-wheat pastry flour or white whole-wheat flour

3 cups all-purpose flour

3 tablespoons baking powder

1 tablespoon baking soda

1 tablespoon kosher salt

1 teaspoon ground cinnamon

In a large bowl, whisk together both flours, the baking powder, baking soda, salt, and cinnamon. Transfer to a large glass jar or other airtight container and store in a cool, dry place for up to 3 months.

EVERYTHING BAGEL SPICE

MAKES: ABOUT ⅓ CUP

PREP TIME: 5 minutes
TOTAL TIME: 5 minutes

Growing up, I never liked everything bagels, but that's probably because I'd never actually had one. Neither of my parents has ever liked onion-flavored anything, so everything bagels never made an appearance at our house. That is, until my brothers started bringing them home—with freshly smeared cream cheese—and life was changed forever. This everything bagel spice brings back all those morning memories. This blend is my go-to when I need to add excitement to an otherwise quiet recipe—it adds so much flavor! I keep a jar in my pantry at all times. Try sprinkling it on the potato pizza (see page 117) or mixing it into salad dressings. You can also sprinkle it on your morning toast, swirl it into hummus, or use it to make seasoned pretzels for your broccoli cheddar soup (see page 94). Feel free to play around with the ratios of ingredients to create a spice that's personalized to you.

2 tablespoons toasted white sesame seeds

1 tablespoon toasted black sesame seeds

2 tablespoons poppy seeds

2 teaspoons granulated onion

2 teaspoons granulated garlic

2 teaspoons flaky sea salt

In a small glass jar with a lid, combine the white and black sesame seeds, poppy seeds, onion, garlic, and salt and mix well. Store at room temperature in a cool, dry place for up to 3 months.

LEMON BASIL PESTO

MAKES: 1 CUP

PREP TIME: 10 minutes
TOTAL TIME: 10 minutes

My best advice? Keep a jar of pesto (homemade or store-bought) on hand at all times. I use basil pesto in many recipes for a quick burst of fresh flavor and a pop of color without having to add a lot of ingredients. Try stirring a few tablespoons into your next pasta dish, adding a spoonful to tomato soup (see page 103), or using it as a sandwich spread for a healthier (and more flavorful) option than traditional mayo. This lemon version has an unexpected extra-special tang that adds a layer of flavor that is missing in traditional pesto.

2 cups packed fresh basil leaves

2 tablespoons toasted nuts or seeds, such as pine nuts, almonds, or raw pumpkin seeds (pepitas)

⅓ cup grated Parmesan cheese

¼ cup extra-virgin olive oil

Zest and juice of 1 lemon

Pinch of crushed red pepper flakes

Kosher salt

In a blender or food processor, combine the basil, nuts, Parmesan, olive oil, lemon zest, lemon juice, and red pepper flakes and pulse until smooth but still a little chunky, about 1 minute. Taste and add salt as needed. Store refrigerated in an airtight container for up to 2 weeks.

PERFECT
PRESSURE COOKER EGGS

4 TO 6 LARGE EGGS

COOK TIME: 2 to 4 minutes,
plus additional time to come to pressure

Cooking eggs isn't always the easiest thing to do. Sometimes I'll end up with a hard-boiled egg that's difficult to peel and a yolk that's dry and crumbly. I've tested many methods in search of the perfect soft- and hard-boiled eggs, and nothing works as well as the Instant Pot. Not only is it quick and incredibly simple to use, the Instant Pot also gives you the egg you're looking for, whether it's soft-boiled, hard-boiled, or something in between. Serve these eggs over your favorite toast, use them to bump up the protein in your next salad, or try them in my dad's cheesy eggs (see page 36).

For Soft-Boiled Eggs: Select high pressure, manual mode, and set to cook for 2 minutes.

For Medium-Boiled Eggs: Select high pressure, manual mode, and set to cook for 3 minutes.

For Hard-Boiled Eggs: Select high pressure, manual mode, and set to cook for 4 minutes.

Place the eggs and 2 cups of water in an electric pressure cooker. Lock the lid in place and cook on high pressure for the desired cooking time. When done cooking, quick or natural release, then open when the pressure subsides. Place the eggs in a bowl of ice water until cool to the touch, about 1 minute. Peel and use as desired.

NO-KNEAD BREAD AND PIZZA DOUGH

....

MAKES: 1 POUND OF DOUGH

....

PREP TIME: 10 minutes
RESTING TIME: 2 hours or overnight
COOK TIME: 45 minutes
TOTAL TIME: 55 minutes,
plus resting time

If you've cooked through my *Half Baked Harvest Cookbook,* you are most likely familiar with its Five-Ingredient Honey Butter Beer Bread. It's a favorite with everyone who's tried it, including my *entire* family. We can't get enough of it. It's the recipe that inspired this dough— yes, the secret ingredient is beer! The beer creates a nice, soft, doughy pizza or an extra-crusty loaf of no-knead bread. I recommend using a beer you love to drink, but truly any kind works. Keep this dough in the fridge to make quick weeknight pizzas or fresh bread any day of the week.

You can let the dough rise overnight at room temperature and in the morning transfer it to the fridge for up to 3 days. Alternately, you can keep the dough in the freezer for up to 3 months. Just thaw the frozen dough overnight in the fridge and use as directed.

3 cups all-purpose flour, plus more as needed (see Note)

2 teaspoons instant yeast

2 teaspoons kosher salt

1 (12-ounce) beer

1 tablespoon extra-virgin olive oil

In a medium bowl, stir together the flour, yeast, and salt. Add the beer and olive oil and mix with a wooden spoon until combined. Cover the bowl with plastic wrap and let sit at room temperature until doubled in size, 1 to 2 hours.

～ TO BAKE AS BREAD ～

1. When ready to bake, place a 6-quart cast-iron Dutch oven or heavy pot on a rack positioned in the center of the oven. Preheat the oven to 450°F. Once it reaches temperature, let the Dutch oven warm for 30 minutes.

2. Turn the dough out onto a generously floured work surface. Using your hands, form the dough into a ball and place it on a large piece of parchment paper.

3. Carefully remove the Dutch oven from the oven and place the dough with the parchment paper in the center of it. Transfer the pot back to the oven, cover, and bake for 30 minutes. Carefully remove the lid and continue baking until the bread is a deep golden brown, about 15 minutes more.

4. Carefully lift the bread out of the pot and place it on a rack to cool completely, about 2 hours. (Don't slice into the bread right out of the oven—you want to let it continue to cook as it cools.)

～ TO USE AS PIZZA DOUGH ～

Turn the dough out onto a floured work surface and divide it into 2 equal pieces. Use half of the dough as directed in any given pizza recipe and save the remaining dough, wrapped in plastic wrap, for another use.

....

To get the right consistency in your dough, start with your base amount of flour, then add more as needed, 1 tablespoon at a time, until the dough is smooth but not dry. It's better to have a dough that's on the slightly sticky side than a dough that's too dry. The dough should be a bit loose; it should not feel dense or heavy.

BREAKFAST &
BRUNCH

BAKED CINNAMON-BUTTER

BRIOCHE FRENCH TOAST

WITH ANY FRUIT JAM

SERVES: 4

PREP TIME: 15 minutes
COOK TIME: 50 minutes
TOTAL TIME: 1 hour, plus chilling time

One year at Christmas I made the mistake of not preparing breakfast the night before, and trust me, I paid the price. Instead of relaxing by the fire on Christmas morning, I played short-order cook at the stove, whipping up French toast all morning long. The lesson? Have a good French toast casserole prepared before Santa arrives. Then all you need to do when you wake up is turn on the oven, throw in the casserole, and wait for it to bake into a buttery, cinnamony, crisp-on-the-edges, soft-on-the-insides French toast casserole. This dish couldn't be easier to prepare and it's truly one of the best breakfasts ever to come out of my kitchen. Dolloping a little cinnamon butter over the bread slices before baking ensures that every bite will be perfectly sweet and spiced with cinnamon. I love serving this topped with a raspberry jam, but if you prepare the Any Fruit Jam you can use whatever is in season, or whatever you love most.

¼ cup pure maple syrup

2 tablespoons brown sugar

4 tablespoons salted butter, melted

8 large eggs, beaten

1 (14-ounce) can full-fat unsweetened coconut milk

3 tablespoons bourbon (optional)

1 tablespoon pure vanilla extract

2 teaspoons ground cinnamon

½ teaspoon kosher salt

1 brioche or challah bread loaf, cut into 8 thick slices

2 tablespoons salted butter, at room temperature

Any Fruit Jam (recipe follows) or store-bought jam, for serving (optional)

Whipped cream, for serving (optional)

1. Grease a 9 × 13 inch-baking dish. In the baking dish, using a fork, mix together the maple syrup, 1 tablespoon of the sugar, and the melted butter.

2. In a large bowl, whisk together the eggs, coconut milk, bourbon (if using), vanilla, 1 teaspoon of the cinnamon, and the salt. Submerge each piece of bread into the egg mixture, allowing them to soak for at least 1 minute. Arrange the bread in the prepared baking dish, and pour the remaining egg mixture evenly over the slices.

3. In a small bowl, using a spatula, combine the 2 tablespoons of softened butter, the remaining 1 tablespoon of sugar, and the remaining 1 teaspoon of cinnamon. Evenly dollop the butter mixture over the bread in the baking dish. Cover with foil or plastic wrap and place in the fridge for 1 hour or up to overnight.

4. When ready to bake, preheat the oven to 375°F.

5. Bake until the French toast is golden and crisp, 45 to 50 minutes. If the tops of the bread begin to brown too quickly, loosely cover the French toast with aluminum foil and continue baking.

6. Serve the French toast warm, topped with jam and whipped cream, if desired.

<10

ANY FRUIT JAM

〜 MAKES: 2 cups 〜

6 cups any fresh fruit

¼ cup pure maple syrup or honey

Juice of 1 lemon

In a medium saucepan, bring the fruit, maple syrup, and lemon juice to a boil over high heat. Use a potato masher or fork to break down the fruit. Continue to cook until the jam has thickened and has been reduced by one-third, 5 to 8 minutes. Remove the pan from the heat and let cool. Store refrigerated in an airtight glass jar for up to 2 weeks.

FRICO AND POLENTA FRIED EGGS

SERVES: 1

PREP TIME: 10 minutes
COOK TIME: 5 minutes
TOTAL TIME: 15 minutes

Are you asking yourself what the heck frico is? Trust me, I've been there. But this is worth knowing: frico is Parmesan cheese that's literally just melted until it's crisp like a cracker. So simple, so delicious. I've taken the classic frico and layered it with polenta and a fried egg for the ultimate easy skillet breakfast . . . or late-night breakfast or dinner if you so please. The key is to cook the cheese first, until it begins to melt and crisp. Then spoon the cooked polenta over the top and crack an egg over the polenta. The cheese will turn golden and crisp while the egg fries up over the polenta. The greens round out the meal and add that ever-important touch of color to your dish.

¼ cup shredded sharp white cheddar cheese

¼ cup grated Parmesan cheese

½ cup cooked creamy polenta, warmed (see Note)

1 tablespoon extra-virgin olive oil

2 large eggs

Kosher salt and freshly ground pepper

1 cup torn Swiss chard, baby kale, or collard greens

Crushed red pepper flakes, for serving

1. In a small bowl, combine the cheddar and Parmesan.

2. Heat a large skillet over medium-low heat. Sprinkle the cheese mixture into two 4-inch rounds in the bottom of the skillet and cook until the cheese starts to melt and become firm, 1 to 2 minutes. Using a small spoon, gently spread the polenta over the cheese rounds and make a well in the center of each polenta mound.

3. Evenly drizzle the olive oil all over the polenta, crack an egg into each well, and season both with salt and pepper. Cook, rotating the skillet occasionally, until the egg whites set around the yolk and begin to crisp at the edges, about 2 minutes. Add the greens around the eggs, cover the skillet, and cook until the greens have wilted, 1 minute more. Remove the skillet from the heat and serve with red pepper flakes.

. . . .

I like to use DeLallo quick-cooking polenta, which only takes 5 minutes, if I don't already have leftover polenta on hand.

BUTTERY CROISSANT STRATA

WITH SPINACH AND PROSCIUTTO

. . . .

SERVES: 8

. . . .

PREP TIME: 15 minutes
COOK TIME: 1 hour
TOTAL TIME: 1 hour, plus chilling and
cooling time

Living up in the mountains with multiple ski resorts just minutes away, we have a lot of guests pass in and out of the house year-round. This casserole has become a go-to when our overnight guests are hungry for brunch. I simply assemble it the night before, pop it in the fridge, and bake it off the next morning. It's so quick and easy to assemble—but the *best* part is how mouthwateringly delicious it is. The croissants are buttery and soft, the eggs are light and fluffy, it's cheesy (duh) and filled with spinach and herbs, and the prosciutto is crisp and salty. It is definitely a step up from grandma's . . . or whoever's recipe you've been using. You can eat the casserole as is, or top it with your favorite fruit jam (see page 24) for a sweet and savory twist. Or if you're like me and love a good breakfast for dinner, this is a really great option, too.

3 tablespoons salted butter, thinly sliced, plus more for greasing

6 croissants, roughly torn into thirds

8 large eggs

3 cups whole milk

1 tablespoon Dijon mustard

1 tablespoon chopped fresh sage

¼ teaspoon freshly grated nutmeg

Kosher salt and freshly ground pepper

12 ounces frozen spinach, thawed and squeezed dry

1½ cups shredded Gouda cheese

1½ cups shredded Gruyère cheese

3 ounces thinly sliced prosciutto, torn

1. Preheat the oven to 350°F. Grease a 9 × 13-inch baking dish.

2. Arrange the croissants in the bottom of the baking dish and cover with the sliced butter. Bake until lightly toasted, 5 to 8 minutes. Remove and let cool in the pan until no longer hot to the touch, about 10 minutes.

3. In a medium bowl, whisk together the eggs, milk, mustard, sage, nutmeg, and a pinch each of salt and pepper. Stir in the spinach and ¾ cup of each cheese. Carefully pour the mixture over the toasted croissants, distributing it evenly. Top with the remaining cheese and add the prosciutto to finish. Cover and refrigerate for at least 30 minutes or overnight.

4. When ready to bake, remove the strata from the fridge and preheat the oven to 350°F.

5. Bake until the center of the strata is set, about 45 minutes. If the croissants begin to brown before the strata is finished cooking, cover with foil and continue baking.

6. Remove the strata from the oven and let cool for 5 minutes before serving.

EGG-IN-A-HOLE WITH TOMATO AND BACON

MAKES: 2 SANDWICHES

PREP TIME: 10 minutes
COOK TIME: 15 minutes
TOTAL TIME: 25 minutes

A classic breakfast sandwich is hard to beat. But I love reinventing the classics, and this sandwich takes the concept to another level. It's like a grilled-cheese and an egg sandwich combined into one. You start by cutting a hole in the bread slices, which makes more room to fill your sandwich with sweet heirloom tomatoes, crispy bacon, and a touch of lemon basil pesto. I love using a good sourdough loaf here or my homemade no-knead bread (see page 20). Sharp cheddar cheese will provide good flavor and melts perfectly over the eggs. If fresh tomatoes aren't in season, use a few oil-packed sun-dried tomatoes, which will be just as delicious.

4 thick slices sourdough or other country-style bread

2 tablespoons salted butter

2 slices thick-cut bacon

4 large eggs

Kosher salt and freshly ground pepper

1 cup shredded sharp cheddar cheese

4 slices heirloom tomatoes

¼ cup Lemon Basil Pesto (page 19) or store-bought pesto

Honey, for serving

1. Using a 2-inch circular cookie cutter, cut 1 circle out of the center of each slice of bread. Discard the circles or snack on them. Spread both sides of the bread evenly with about 1 tablespoon of the butter.

2. Place a large skillet over medium heat. Add the bacon and cook until the fat renders and the bacon is crispy, about 5 minutes. Remove the bacon from the skillet and drain on a paper towel–lined plate.

3. In the same skillet, melt the remaining 1 tablespoon of butter over medium heat. Working in batches as needed, add the bread slices and cook until toasted and golden on the bottom, 2 to 3 minutes. Flip the toast and crack an egg into the center hole of each piece of bread. Season with salt and pepper and cook 2 to 3 minutes more, flip again, and sprinkle each piece of bread with cheese. Cover the pan and cook until the cheese has melted and the egg is cooked to your liking, 30 seconds to 1 minute. Remove from the skillet.

4. To assemble, layer the bacon, tomatoes, and pesto on the cheese side of two slices of bread and drizzle with honey. Top each with another slice of bread, cheese side down, being careful not to break the egg. Serve immediately.

AVOCADO BREAKFAST TACOS

WITH CRISPY SHALLOTS AND CHIPOTLE SALSA

SERVES: 2

PREP TIME: 10 minutes
COOK TIME: 15 minutes
TOTAL TIME: 25 minutes

Like most, I love a good breakfast taco. I prefer them with soft scrambled eggs, cheese, and a good amount of spicy salsa. This is my "weekday" version—they are ideal for someone who loves flavor and texture but doesn't necessarily have a whole lot of time. All made in a single skillet, the eggs are scrambled with cheddar cheese and topped with bacon, crispy shallots, and smoky chipotle salsa. You can certainly skip the bacon if it's not your thing, but I beg you, do not skip those crispy shallots.

4 large eggs

Kosher salt and freshly ground pepper

3 slices thick-cut bacon, chopped, for serving

2 shallots, thinly sliced, for serving

1 tablespoon salted butter

½ cup shredded cheddar cheese

4 corn or flour tortillas, warmed

1 cup roughly chopped fresh spinach or baby kale

1 avocado, sliced

2 green onions, chopped, for serving

Lime wedges, for serving

Chipotle Salsa (recipe follows) or store-bought salsa, for serving

1. In a medium bowl, whisk together the eggs and a pinch each of salt and pepper.

2. Place a large skillet over medium heat. Add the bacon and cook until the fat renders and the bacon is crispy, about 5 minutes. Remove the bacon from the skillet and drain on a paper towel–lined plate. Lightly crumble the bacon with your hands.

3. Place the shallots in the same skillet and cook over medium heat, stirring occasionally, until caramelized, about 3 minutes. Remove the shallots from the skillet and drain on the paper towel–lined plate. The shallots will crisp up as they dry.

4. Wipe out the skillet and melt the butter in it over medium heat. Add the beaten eggs and cook, undisturbed, until a thin white layer forms around the edge of the skillet. Using a rubber spatula, gently push the eggs around the skillet until fluffy and barely set, about 2 minutes. Immediately transfer the eggs to a plate and gently fold in the cheese.

5. To assemble, on the warmed tortillas layer the greens, eggs, and avocado. Top with the bacon, shallots, and green onions. Serve with lime wedges and salsa alongside.

<10

CHIPOTLE SALSA

MAKES: about 1½ cups

1 (14-ounce) can fire-roasted diced tomatoes

¼ cup chipotle peppers in adobo

2 tablespoons toasted sesame seeds

Kosher salt

In a blender or food processor, pulse together the tomatoes and chipotle peppers until mostly smooth, about 1 minute. Add the sesame seeds and season with salt. Pulse to combine, about 30 seconds. Taste and add more salt as needed. Store refrigerated in an airtight container for up to 2 weeks.

If you don't have Everyday Pancake Mix on hand, combine 1½ cups all-purpose flour, 2 teaspoons baking powder, and 1 teaspoon kosher salt instead.

PUMPKIN BUTTER CRÈME FRAÎCHE PANCAKES

WITH WHIPPED MAPLE BUTTER

· · · · · · · · · ·

SERVES: 4

· · · · · · · · · ·

PREP TIME: 10 minutes
RESTING TIME: 10 minutes or overnight
COOK TIME: 10 minutes
TOTAL TIME: 20 minutes,
plus chilling time

Everyone who knows me, even just a little, knows that fall is *my* season. The months of September through December are my favorites, and as soon as October rolls around I'm breaking out the autumn-y spices. Pumpkin pancakes are one of the first dishes I turn to. To make things easy, I use my everyday pancake mix as a base and add store-bought pumpkin butter and rich crème fraîche for a version that feels extra fancy but that, in reality, is super easy—you can even make the batter the night before. Enjoy the pancakes as they are, or finish them off with a little whipped maple butter for a touch of buttery sweetness. (I highly recommend the butter—it's life changing.)

¾ cup pumpkin butter

½ cup crème fraîche

2 large eggs

3 tablespoons salted butter, melted, plus more for the pan

1½ cups whole milk

1½ cups Everyday Pancake Mix (page 17)

Whipped Maple Butter (recipe follows), for serving

Maple syrup, for serving (optional)

1. In a large bowl, whisk together the pumpkin butter, crème fraîche, eggs, melted butter, and milk. Fold in the pancake mix until just combined. Cover and let sit for 10 minutes at room temperature or refrigerate overnight.

2. Preheat the oven to 150°F.

3. In a large skillet or griddle, melt 1 tablespoon of butter over medium heat. Pour ¼ cup of the pancake batter into the skillet. Cook until bubbles appear on the surface, about 2 minutes, then use a spatula to gently flip the pancake. Cook on the second side until golden, about 1 minute more. Transfer the pancake to a baking dish and keep warm in the oven.

4. Repeat with the remaining batter, adding more butter to the skillet, if needed.

5. To serve, spread each pancake with a bit of maple butter. Serve with maple syrup alongside, if desired.

· <10   ·

WHIPPED MAPLE BUTTER

∼ MAKES: ½ cup ∼

½ cup (1 stick) salted butter

¼ cup pure maple syrup

1. In a small saucepan, melt the butter over medium heat, stirring occasionally, until the butter is lightly browned, 3 to 5 minutes. Transfer the butter to the bowl of a stand mixer. Chill in the fridge for 20 minutes.

2. Add the maple syrup to the butter. Using the whisk attachment, whip the chilled butter and syrup together on medium-high speed until light and fluffy, 1 to 2 minutes. Store refrigerated in an airtight container for up to 2 weeks.

DAD'S CHEESY EGGS

SERVES: 2

PREP TIME: 5 minutes
COOK TIME: 3 minutes
TOTAL TIME: 8 minutes, plus
additional time to come to pressure

My mom and dad have been married since they were eighteen and twenty-one, respectively. My dad played college hockey, and the games were often late at night. When they returned home in the early morning hours, he would make my mom these cheesy eggs with a side of toast. My mom would have that eyes-rolling reaction of delight that's become one of the reasons I love to cook. This recipe is quite simply eggs and cheese, but sometimes it's the most basic things that are the most perfect—that's definitely the case with these eggs.

4 warm medium-boiled eggs
(see page 19)

½ cup finely shredded cheddar cheese

Kosher salt and freshly ground pepper

Buttered toast, for serving

1 tablespoon chopped fresh chives and/or basil, for serving

Crushed red pepper flakes, for serving

1. In a medium bowl, gently mash together the warm eggs and cheese with a fork. Season to taste with salt and red pepper.

2. Spread the mixture onto the buttered toast and top with chives and a pinch of red pepper flakes.

Make sure your eggs are warm when you mix them with the cheese. Their heat is what melts the cheese, which is key. If the cheese is not melting, stick the toast under the broiler for a few seconds to get everything warm and delicious.

BLUEBERRY LEMON PULL-APART BREAD

MAKES: 2 PULL-APART LOAVES

PREP TIME: 15 minutes
COOK TIME: 45 minutes
TOTAL TIME: 1 hour, plus rising time

As soon as the days begin to get longer and the winter chill has just about worn off, I love to make this bread. It screams warmer spring days: it's bright, beautiful, hinted with fresh lemony flavor, and bursting with sweet blueberries. A drizzle of thyme-infused honey and a smear of salted butter give this bread the perfect finish. It's just as good for breakfast as it is for an after-dinner dessert. I prefer mine in the afternoon, with a mug of tea and a good book, but you can enjoy it any time of day.

Butter, for greasing

4 ounces crème fraîche

¼ cup plus 1 tablespoon honey

2 teaspoons pure vanilla extract

Zest and juice of 1 lemon

½ teaspoon ground cinnamon

Everyday Bread Dough, at room temperature (page 16)

2 cups fresh or frozen blueberries

1 tablespoon fresh thyme leaves

1. Grease two 9 × 5-inch loaf pans.

2. **Make the filling.** In a small bowl, stir together the crème fraîche, 1 tablespoon of the honey, the vanilla, lemon zest, lemon juice, and cinnamon.

3. **Make the rolls.** Turn out the dough onto a lightly floured work surface, punch it down, and roll it into a 10 × 16-inch rectangle about ½ inch thick, with a long side facing you. Spread the crème fraîche mixture over the dough and sprinkle the blueberries evenly on top. Starting with the long edge closest to you, pull the dough up and over the filling and carefully roll it into a log, keeping it fairly tight. Pinch the edge to seal.

4. Turn the log seam side down and cut it into 12 equal rolls. Place 6 rolls, seam side down, in each prepared pan; the rolls should touch. Cover and let rise in a warm place until almost doubled in size, 30 minutes to 1 hour.

5. Preheat the oven to 350°F.

6. Bake the rolls until lightly browned on top, 45 to 50 minutes. Set aside to cool slightly.

7. **Make the thyme honey.** Meanwhile, combine the thyme and the remaining ¼ cup of honey in a small saucepan over low heat. Simmer until the honey begins to bubble, about 3 minutes, and remove the pan from the heat.

8. Drizzle the bread with the warm thyme honey. Store any leftovers refrigerated in an airtight container for up to 3 days.

. . . .

This recipe makes enough for two loaves of bread. Bake them both, or freeze one for later. To freeze, wrap the baked bread in plastic wrap and freeze for up to 3 months. Thaw overnight on the counter, add the thyme honey, and enjoy!

MAPLE-GLAZED CARDAMOM APPLE FRITTERS

....

MAKES: 12 TO 14 FRITTERS

....

PREP TIME: 30 minutes
COOK TIME: 15 minutes
TOTAL TIME: 45 minutes, plus rising time

When apples come into season, the first thing I make with them are these fritters. Because, let's be honest, nothing is better than an apple fritter on a crisp fall day—especially when using freshly picked apples. To keep these "super simple," I use my everyday bread dough and mix in Honeycrisp apples (my favorite) and ground cardamom (for some spice). Drizzle each light and airy fritter with a vanilla-maple glaze and enjoy with hot coffee in hand. They make the perfect early morning or late afternoon treat. These fritters are best eaten the day they are made, so invite friends over for brunch or package up any leftovers and gift a few warm fritters to your neighbors for serious bonus points.

CARDAMOM APPLE FILLING

2 tablespoons salted butter

2 large apples, cored and chopped (I like Honeycrisp)

1½ teaspoons ground cinnamon

½ teaspoon ground cardamom

3 tablespoons pure maple syrup

MAPLE GLAZE

¼ cup pure maple syrup

¼ cup confectioners' sugar

FRITTERS

Everyday Bread Dough, at room temperature (page 16)

⅓ cup apple butter

Neutral oil, such as canola or vegetable oil, for frying

1 teaspoon pure vanilla extract

1. **Make the filling.** Melt the butter in a large skillet over medium heat. Add the apples, cinnamon, and cardamom and cook, stirring occasionally, until tender, 5 minutes. Add the maple syrup and continue cooking until the apples are caramelized, 3 to 5 minutes more. Remove the skillet from the heat and let cool slightly.

2. **Make the dough.** On a lightly floured work surface, roll the dough into a rectangle about 10 × 16 inches and ½ inch thick. Spread the apple butter over the dough and arrange the caramelized apples over the top. Starting with the long edge closest to you, pull the dough up and over the filling and carefully roll the dough into a log, keeping it fairly tight. Pinch the edge to seal. Rotate the log of dough so it's perpendicular to your body. Roll the dough out into a ½-inch-thick rectangle; don't worry if any apples pop out—just push them back.

3. Cut the dough into 12 to 14 squares and arrange them on a parchment-lined baking sheet. Cover with plastic wrap and let rise in a warm place until puffed and slightly rounded, 15 to 30 minutes.

4. **Cook the fritters.** In a large saucepan over medium heat, bring about 2 inches of oil to 350°F. Carefully lower 3 or 4 fritters at a time into the hot oil. Fry until golden, 1 to 2 minutes, then flip and fry until golden brown on the other side, 1 to 2 minutes more. Transfer the fritters from the oil to a paper towel–lined baking sheet to cool slightly.

5. **Make the glaze.** In a medium bowl, whisk together the maple syrup, confectioners' sugar, and vanilla.

6. Drizzle the glaze over the warm fritters. Serve immediately. Store any leftovers refrigerated in an airtight container for up to 2 days.

....

Save yourself time by leaving the skin on the apples. I love the added texture and flavor.

COCONUT-BANANA MUFFINS

MAKES: 12 MUFFINS

PREP TIME: 15 minutes
COOK TIME: about 20 minutes
TOTAL TIME: about 35 minutes

Everyone needs a good banana muffin recipe in their back pocket—how else are you going to use up all those slowly ripening bananas on the kitchen counter? These are the ideal on-the-go breakfast, midday snack, or packable lunchbox item. I like to fold mini chocolate chips into the batter and top off each muffin with coconut streusel. The streusel might not seem necessary, but it is sweet and a little crunchy, and it really takes these muffins up a notch from the ones at your local bakery. If you have time on Sunday, bake up a batch of these to enjoy that morning or to pack up and take with you throughout the week.

½ cup (1 stick) salted butter, melted

¼ cup honey

2 teaspoons pure vanilla extract

2 large eggs

3 or 4 very ripe bananas, mashed (1 cup mashed banana)

¼ cup whole milk

2¼ cups plus 2 tablespoons all-purpose flour

2 teaspoons baking powder

½ teaspoon baking soda

1¾ teaspoons ground cinnamon

1 cup mini chocolate chips (optional)

1 cup unsweetened flaked coconut

3 tablespoons cold salted butter, cubed

1. Preheat the oven to 350°F. Line a 12-cup muffin tin with paper liners.

2. In a large bowl, combine the melted butter, honey, and vanilla. Add the eggs, one at a time, and stir until fully incorporated. Add the mashed bananas and milk and stir until mixed well. Add 2¼ cups of the flour, the baking powder, baking soda, and ¾ teaspoon of the cinnamon and stir until just combined. Fold in the chocolate chips (if using). Divide the batter evenly among the muffin cups, filling each three-quarters of the way.

3. In a medium bowl, combine the coconut, the remaining 2 tablespoons of flour, and the remaining 1 teaspoon of cinnamon. Add the butter and work together with your hands until a crumbly mixture forms. Sprinkle the streusel over the batter, dividing it evenly.

4. Bake until a toothpick inserted into the center of a muffin comes out clean, 20 to 22 minutes. Serve the muffins warm or at room temperature. Store any leftovers at room temperature in an airtight container for up to 5 days.

OVERNIGHT
CINNAMON ROLL BREAD

WITH CHAI FROSTING

. . . .

MAKES: 1 (9 × 5-INCH) LOAF

. . . .

PREP TIME: 1 hour
COOK TIME: about 35 minutes
TOTAL TIME: 1 hour 30 minutes,
plus rising and cooling time

Homemade cinnamon rolls are always impressive, but switching things up and turning your rolls into a beautiful bread keeps things simple and easy, but every bit as delicious. And the chai frosting? It's as good as it sounds. Not too sweet, spiced just right—when drizzled over this swirly cinnamon bread, it melts into every nook and cranny. I let the dough rise overnight in the fridge and bake it in the morning. It's perfect for a holiday breakfast or weekend morning treat.

CINNAMON ROLLS

6 tablespoons very softened salted butter, plus more for greasing

¾ cup packed light brown sugar

1½ teaspoons ground cinnamon

Basic Everyday Bread Dough, at room temperature (page 16)

CHAI FROSTING

4 ounces cream cheese, at room temperature

4 tablespoons salted butter, at room temperature

1½ teaspoons pure vanilla extract

1½ cups confectioners' sugar

½ teaspoon ground cinnamon

¼ teaspoon ground allspice

¼ teaspoon ground ginger

¼ teaspoon ground cardamom

1. **Make the rolls.** Butter a 9 × 5-inch loaf pan and line with parchment paper. In a small bowl, combine the brown sugar and cinnamon and set aside.

2. When the dough has doubled in size, turn it out onto a lightly floured work surface, punch it down, and roll it into a ball using your hands. Roll the dough into a rectangle (approximately 12 × 18 inches). Spread the softened butter over the dough and sprinkle it with the cinnamon sugar. Starting with the edge of dough closest to you, roll the dough into a log, keeping it tight as you go. Pinch along the edges of the log to seal it.

3. Cut the log into 6 rolls and place them cut side up in the prepared pan. Cover and let rise 45 minutes to 1 hour in a warm place or up to overnight in the fridge. Bring the dough to room temperature before baking.

4. Preheat the oven to 350°F. Place the pan on a rimmed baking sheet and bake until browned on top, 30 to 35 minutes. If the bread is browning too quickly, cover it with foil. Let cool 5 minutes before turning it out onto a rack.

5. **Make the frosting.** In the bowl of a stand mixer fitted with the paddle attachment or in a medium bowl with an electric hand mixer, beat together the cream cheese, butter, and vanilla until fluffy. Gradually beat in the confectioners' sugar, cinnamon, allspice, ginger, and cardamom until combined.

6. Spread the frosting over the warm bread. Serve immediately. Store any leftovers refrigerated in an airtight container for up to 3 days.

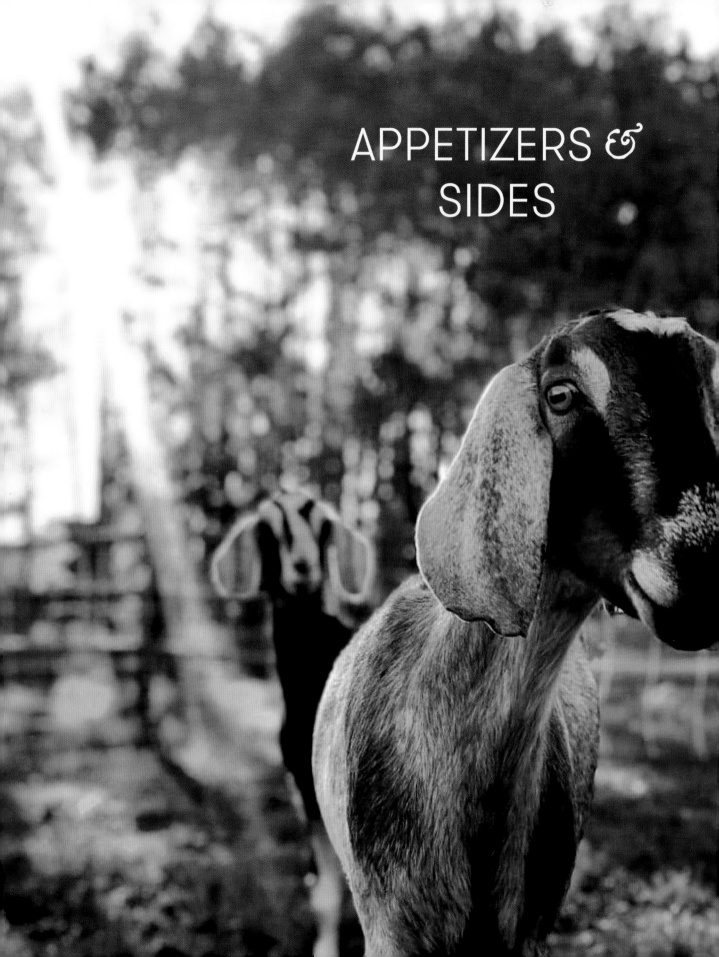

APPETIZERS &
SIDES

CHEESY POBLANO AND BACON QUESADILLA

....
SERVES: 4
....

PREP TIME: 10 minutes
COOK TIME: 20 minutes
TOTAL TIME: 30 minutes

This is the best quesadilla *ever*. I know, that statement is bold, but this one really is my favorite. It's cheesy and smoky (thanks to the poblano peppers) and it has a nice bacon flavor. I serve it topped with a sweet pineapple salsa that really complements the other flavors and almost makes you feel like you're enjoying a quesadilla on a beach somewhere, which is really nice for me, considering it's winter for basically nine months out of the year where I live in Colorado. This quesadilla comes together in no time, making it perfect for a quick lunch or even dinner, especially when served with a side salad.

4 slices thick-cut bacon, quartered

2 poblano peppers, seeded and thinly sliced

8 large flour tortillas

1 cup shredded pepper Jack cheese

1 cup fresh baby spinach, roughly chopped

1 cup shredded cheddar cheese

2 tablespoons extra-virgin olive oil

Pickled Jalapeño Pineapple Salsa (recipe follows) or store-bought salsa, for serving

1. Place the bacon in a cold large skillet over medium heat. Cook until the fat renders and the bacon is crisp, 4 to 5 minutes. Transfer the bacon to a paper towel–lined plate to drain, reserving the fat in the skillet.

2. Return the skillet to the heat, add the poblanos, and cook until soft, about 5 minutes. Transfer the peppers to a small bowl.

3. Lay out 4 tortillas on a clean work surface. Sprinkle each with ¼ cup of the pepper Jack cheese, then evenly divide the spinach, peppers, and bacon among the 4 tortillas. Finish each with ¼ cup of the cheddar cheese and another tortilla.

4. Wipe out the skillet and heat the olive oil over medium heat. When the oil shimmers, add the quesadillas, one at a time. Cook until the bottom is crispy and golden brown, about 2 minutes, then gently flip and cook until the tortilla is golden and the cheese has melted, 2 to 3 minutes more.

5. Serve hot with salsa alongside.

.... <10 ....

PICKLED JALAPEÑO PINEAPPLE SALSA

~ MAKES: 2 cups ~

2 cups fresh pineapple chunks

2 tablespoons chopped pickled jalapeño peppers

Juice of 1 lime

⅓ cup fresh cilantro, chopped

Flaky sea salt

In a medium bowl, stir together the pineapple, jalapeño, lime juice, cilantro, and a pinch of salt. Store the salsa refrigerated in an airtight container for up to 2 days.

RICOTTA TOAST

WITH HONEY-ROASTED GRAPES

SERVES: 6

PREP TIME: 10 minutes
COOK TIME: 20 minutes
TOTAL TIME: 30 minutes

Grapes can be used in so many dishes but are so often neglected. And if you've never roasted them before, now is the time. Seriously, right now. Grab a bunch of grapes (I prefer red for roasting), toss them with honey and fresh thyme, and roast away. As the grapes heat up, they begin to caramelize and release their juices. They're juicy, sweet, a little savory, and best enjoyed when spooned over a piece of crusty ricotta toast and finished with a dusting of flaky sea salt. Super simple, super good. For a fancy touch, I add a drizzle of balsamic vinegar—but that's definitely not a must; this toast is delicious on its own.

2 cups red grapes, halved if large

¼ cup honey

1 tablespoon salted butter

Flaky sea salt

6 slices rustic or whole-grain bread, toasted

1 cup whole-milk ricotta cheese

White balsamic or balsamic vinegar, for drizzling (optional)

2 tablespoons fresh thyme leaves, for garnish

1. Preheat the oven to 425°F.

2. In a 9 × 13-inch baking dish, combine the grapes, honey, butter, and a pinch of salt. Bake until the grapes begin to blister, 15 to 20 minutes. Set aside to cool slightly.

3. Meanwhile, spread each piece of toasted bread with the ricotta, dividing it evenly. Spoon the roasted grapes over the ricotta and top each piece with a drizzle of vinegar (if using), thyme, and flaky salt.

THREE-INGREDIENT
BLUE CHEESE BITES

SERVES: 8

PREP TIME: 10 minutes
COOK TIME: 20 minutes
TOTAL TIME: 30 minutes

Without a doubt, this is the easiest recipe I've ever made. It's also one that's been in my family for as long as I can remember—one my grandma would make anytime she had a party. You need only three simple ingredients: store-bought biscuit dough, butter, and blue cheese. Usually I recommend making your own biscuits, but for this recipe, store-bought dough is the only way to go. It just works, and sometimes it's okay to take a little shortcut. I've yet to meet anyone who doesn't love this appetizer—and it's great for entertaining year-round.

For this recipe in particular, I recommend using a 4-ounce package of pre-crumbled blue cheese. This will be less "stinky" and tends to go over better in a crowd. Alternately, if you really hate blue cheese, you can use feta, but I encourage you to give the blue cheese a try first.

½ cup (1 stick) salted butter

1 (12-ounce) can flaky biscuit dough

4 ounces crumbled blue cheese

Fresh parsley or thyme leaves, roughly chopped, for garnish (optional)

1. Preheat the oven to 375°F.

2. Place the butter in a 9-inch glass pie plate and microwave to melt.

3. Separate the dough into individual biscuits and cut each into quarters. Place the pieces in the pie plate and toss to coat with the butter. Sprinkle the blue cheese evenly over the dough.

4. Bake until the top is lightly browned and bubbly, 15 to 20 minutes. Top with fresh parsley, if desired, and serve.

BURRATA WITH PEPPERONATA AND TOMATOES

SERVES: 6

PREP TIME: 10 minutes
COOK TIME: 15 minutes
TOTAL TIME: 25 minutes

Pepperonata—a mix of sautéed bell peppers, olive oil, garlic, and herbs—is common in Italian cooking and is traditionally served over meats and seafood. I add sweet cherry tomatoes to the condiment and spoon it over fresh burrata cheese for an appetizer that's light, colorful, and tasty. For the best flavor, use a mix of colored bell peppers and be sure to serve your favorite toasted bread and crackers alongside for easy dipping and scooping. My best tip? Make a double batch and keep any extra in an airtight container in the fridge for up to 1 week. Add it to sandwiches or a cheese board, or even toss it with plain pasta for a fast dinner.

⅓ cup extra-virgin olive oil

3 red, yellow, or orange bell peppers, seeded and thinly sliced

2 cups cherry tomatoes

2 garlic cloves, smashed

2 tablespoons fresh thyme leaves

1 tablespoon fresh oregano leaves

1 tablespoon balsamic vinegar

Pinch of crushed red pepper flakes

Pinch of kosher salt

8 ounces burrata cheese

Fresh basil leaves, for garnish

Crackers or toasted bread, for serving

1. Heat a medium skillet over medium heat. Add the olive oil, bell peppers, tomatoes, garlic, thyme, oregano, vinegar, red pepper flakes, and salt and stir to combine. Cook until the bell peppers are soft and the garlic is fragrant, about 15 minutes. Remove the skillet from the heat.

2. Arrange the burrata on a serving plate and spoon the pepperonata around the cheese. Top with the basil leaves. Serve with crackers or toasted bread alongside.

HERB-AND-GARLIC
PULL-APART ROLLS

MAKES: 12 ROLLS

PREP TIME: 15 minutes
COOK TIME: 20 minutes
TOTAL TIME: 35 minutes, plus rising time

Having a good roll recipe that goes with just about any meal is essential for your arsenal. Rolls are one of those side dishes that pretty much everyone loves. These are my go-to for Sunday night dinners or holidays with family. Start with my basic everyday bread dough, add garlic, and then bake into fluffy rolls. As soon as you take the rolls out of the oven, begin to make the herb garlic butter on the stove. The herbs infuse the butter while the garlic caramelizes, turning soft and buttery. Brush the butter over each roll for delicious flavor. They're sure to become a new favorite for *your* family and friends, too!

PULL-APART ROLLS

Basic Everyday Bread Dough (page 16)

1 garlic clove, grated

HERB GARLIC BUTTER

4 tablespoons salted butter, plus more for greasing

3 garlic cloves, grated

1 tablespoon Italian seasoning

¼ cup grated Parmesan cheese

Kosher salt (optional)

Fresh basil or oregano leaves, torn, for serving

1. Preheat the oven to 350°F. Grease a 9 × 13-inch baking dish.

2. **Make the rolls.** Prepare the basic everyday bread dough, adding the grated garlic to the dough when combining in the stand mixer.

3. Lightly dust a work surface with flour. Turn out the dough, punch it down, and divide it into 12 equal balls. Arrange the dough balls in the prepared baking dish. Cover the dish with plastic wrap and let the rolls rise in a warm place until puffy and almost doubled in size, about 20 minutes.

4. Bake the rolls until their tops are golden brown, about 20 minutes.

5. **Make the butter.** In a small skillet, melt the butter over low heat. Add the garlic and Italian seasoning and cook over low heat until the butter is lightly browned and the garlic is golden, about 3 minutes. Remove the skillet from the heat and stir in the Parmesan.

6. Brush the rolls with the warm herb garlic butter and sprinkle with salt, if desired. Sprinkle with fresh basil to garnish. Pull them apart and serve warm.

OVEN-BAKED
CAJUN FRIES

SERVES: 4

PREP TIME: 15 minutes
COOK TIME: 40 minutes
TOTAL TIME: 55 minutes

When I was a kid, my dad would often make fries in the oven. It's the one food all of us kids would eat . . . because who doesn't love potatoes? I adopted his exact cooking method, but since I also love a little spice, I added some fresh thyme, Creole seasoning, and a good amount of paprika. Addictive! The key to a good oven-fry, though? Leave those skins on your potatoes! Not only does this make your life so much easier (read: no peeling!) but the skin of the potato becomes perfectly crispy. You'll end up with a better, much more rustic oven-fry. Plus, the word on the street is that the potato skin holds the most nutrients.

4 medium russet potatoes, cut into ¼-inch sticks

¼ cup extra-virgin olive oil

2 tablespoons fresh thyme leaves

2 teaspoons Homemade Creole Seasoning (recipe follows) or store-bought blend

2 teaspoons smoked paprika

½ teaspoon ground cayenne pepper

Flaky sea salt

1. Preheat the oven to 425°F.

2. Place the potatoes on a large rimmed baking sheet (or two, if needed), making sure not to overcrowd the pan. Drizzle with olive oil and season with the thyme, Creole seasoning, paprika, cayenne, and a large pinch of salt. Gently toss to coat and spread out evenly.

3. Bake for 15 to 20 minutes, until golden, flip, and bake until deeply golden and crispy, 15 to 20 minutes more.

4. Serve hot with additional salt as needed.

<10

HOMEMADE CREOLE SEASONING

MAKES: ¾ cup

2½ tablespoons smoked paprika

2 tablespoons garlic powder

1½ tablespoons kosher salt

1 tablespoon freshly ground black pepper

1 tablespoon onion powder

1 tablespoon ground cayenne pepper

1 tablespoon dried oregano

1 tablespoon dried thyme

Combine all ingredients until well mixed. Store at room temperature in an airtight container in a cool, dry place for up to 3 months.

BALSAMIC PEACH AND BRIE TART

WITH CRISPY PROSCIUTTO

SERVES: 6

PREP TIME: 10 minutes
COOK TIME: 30 minutes
TOTAL TIME: 40 minutes

Quite honestly, the title of this recipe says it all. Flaky puff pastry, melted Brie, roasted peaches, and crispy prosciutto. It's sweet, savory, and salty, and it fulfills just about every craving you could possibly have. Best part? It couldn't be simpler. Serve this as an appetizer or mix up a light arugula salad (see page 80) and serve it atop the tart for an easy summertime dinner.

1 sheet frozen puff pastry, thawed

⅓ cup Lemon Basil Pesto (page 19) or store-bought pesto

1 (8-ounce) wheel Brie cheese, rind on and sliced into ⅛-inch slices

2 ripe peaches, thinly sliced (see Note)

Extra-virgin olive oil

Kosher salt and freshly ground pepper

3 ounces thinly sliced prosciutto, torn

¼ cup balsamic vinegar

2 to 3 tablespoons honey

Fresh basil leaves, for serving

1. Preheat the oven to 425°F. Line a rimmed baking sheet with parchment paper.

2. Gently roll the puff pastry out on a clean work surface to a ⅛-inch thickness and transfer it to the prepared baking sheet. Prick the pastry all over with a fork, then spread the pesto evenly over the dough, leaving a ½-inch border. Arrange the Brie and peaches on top of the pesto and drizzle lightly with olive oil. Season with salt and pepper and top with the prosciutto. Sprinkle the edges of the dough with pepper.

3. Bake until the pastry is golden and the prosciutto is crisp, 25 to 30 minutes.

4. Meanwhile, in a small bowl, whisk together the vinegar and honey.

5. Remove the tart from the oven, top with basil leaves, and drizzle with the honey mixture. Cut into pieces and serve warm.

If peaches are not in season, I love using apples or cranberries. In the springtime, opt for strawberries or blueberries. If you're using cranberries or blueberries, I recommend omitting the prosciutto.

THE BEST PRESSURE COOKER MASHED POTATOES

SERVES: 6

PREP TIME: 10 minutes
COOK TIME: 10 minutes, plus additional
time to come to pressure
TOTAL TIME: 20 minutes

Everyone should know how to whip up a good bowl of mashed potatoes. In my family, there's probably not a more loved side dish. If there were ever to be a vote, potatoes would surely win. What I'm trying to say is, you need to know how to make mashed potatoes, and this is the recipe that will become your go-to. Just throw everything into the pressure cooker, let it do its thing, mash the potatoes, brown some butter with fresh sage, put it all together, and done. No standing at the stove dealing with an overflowing pot, no fancy peeling methods, and it's ready in less than half an hour—with most of that time hands-off. Easy, foolproof, and, of course, delicious.

8 medium Yukon gold potatoes, peeled if desired

4 garlic cloves, smashed

1 teaspoon kosher salt

Freshly ground pepper

¾ cup whole milk or heavy cream

½ cup grated Parmesan cheese

2 tablespoons mascarpone cheese

6 tablespoons salted butter

1 tablespoon chopped fresh sage leaves

1. In the pressure cooker pot, combine the potatoes, garlic, salt, and a pinch of pepper, and cover with 3 to 4 cups of water to submerge the potatoes.

2. Lock the lid in place and cook on high pressure for 10 minutes. Quick or natural release, then open when the pressure subsides. Drain the potatoes and add them back to the pressure cooker pot. Add the milk and mash, using a potato masher or a hand mixer, until smooth and creamy. Stir in the Parmesan and mascarpone until combined.

3. Meanwhile, in a small skillet, melt the butter over medium heat until just browned, whisking the browned bits off the bottom of the pan, about 3 minutes. Stir in the sage and cook until fragrant, about 30 seconds. Pour the browned butter into the warm mashed potatoes and stir to combine. Taste and add more salt and pepper as needed.

CACIO E PEPE BRUSSELS SPROUTS

. . . .

SERVES: 6

. . . .

PREP TIME: 10 minutes
COOK TIME: 5 minutes
TOTAL TIME: 15 minutes

This recipe is for the cheese lover who wants to love Brussels sprouts, but doesn't . . . yet. *Cacio e pepe* translates from Italian to "cheese and pepper" and traditionally is served as a pasta. To create a lighter dish, I swapped the pasta for shredded sprouts and tossed them with a generous amount of grated cheese, butter, pepper, lemon, and even some toasted nuts for a nice little crunch. Save yourself time by buying shredded Brussels sprouts and this dish will come together in minutes. It's a great side, or you can serve it as a main, alongside a fried egg and creamy polenta. Mmmm!

2 tablespoons extra-virgin olive oil

1½ teaspoons freshly ground pepper

Crushed red pepper flakes

1 (12-ounce) bag shredded Brussels sprouts (see Note)

2 tablespoons salted butter

1 teaspoon kosher salt

1½ cups grated Parmesan cheese, plus more for serving

Zest of 1 lemon

⅓ cup toasted hazelnuts or pecans, roughly chopped

1. In a large skillet over medium heat, cook the olive oil, pepper, and red pepper flakes together until toasted, 30 seconds to 1 minute. Add the Brussels sprouts and cook, without stirring, until they begin to soften, about 2 minutes.

2. Stir in the butter, season with the salt, and cook until the Brussels sprouts just begin to char, about 2 minutes. Remove the skillet from the heat and add the Parmesan, lemon zest, and hazelnuts.

3. Serve warm, topped with more fresh Parmesan.

. . . .

You can carefully shave your own Brussels sprouts using a mandoline, but buying them already prepped is a major time-saver.

PROSCIUTTO-WRAPPED
ZUCCHINI BITES
WITH GOAT CHEESE AND THYME

MAKES: 18 TO 20 ROLLS

PREP TIME: 20 minutes
COOK TIME: about 20 minutes
TOTAL TIME: 40 minutes, plus cooling time

Looking for an appetizer alternative to the oh-so-average pizza bites or pigs in a blanket? Look no further. These are so much more flavorful, are healthier, and best of all . . . they're easy! The prosciutto will be crispy, the cheese will be melty, and in the end, you'll have delicious little bites that are the perfect appetizer or snack. I promise, these are definitely better than any apps from the freezer section of the grocery store.

4 small or 2 medium zucchini, sliced lengthwise into very thin ribbons

1 tablespoon extra-virgin olive oil

Kosher salt and freshly ground pepper

6 ounces goat cheese (see Note)

1 tablespoon fresh thyme, plus more for serving

2 teaspoons honey, plus more for serving

Zest of ½ lemon

¼ cup sun-dried tomatoes packed in oil, drained and chopped

¼ cup fresh basil leaves, chopped

10 thin slices prosciutto, sliced in half lengthwise

1. Preheat the oven to 425°F. Line a rimmed baking sheet with parchment paper.

2. In a large bowl, toss the zucchini ribbons with olive oil and a pinch each of salt and pepper.

3. In a small bowl, stir together the goat cheese, thyme, honey, lemon zest, sun-dried tomatoes, basil, and a pinch each of salt and pepper.

4. Working with one at a time, lay out a zucchini ribbon on a clean work surface. Spoon 1 tablespoon of the cheese mixture onto one end and roll up the ribbon. Wrap a piece of prosciutto around the zucchini to secure. Place the rolls seam side down on the prepared baking sheet. Repeat with the remaining zucchini ribbons.

5. Bake until the prosciutto is crisp, 20 to 25 minutes. The rolls are going to ooze a bit; this is okay. Let them set up on the baking sheet for 6 minutes before serving them sprinkled with fresh thyme and drizzled with honey.

You can totally use ricotta here if that is more your thing.

EXTRA-SMOOTH HUMMUS

SERVES: 8

PREP TIME: 10 minutes
COOK TIME: See specific device method

Hummus isn't always my first idea when it comes to appetizers and snacks—I tend to sway toward a good cheese board. But this easy pressure cooker version has me hooked. It's been on heavy repeat in my kitchen, so I knew I had to share it. Cooking the chickpeas in the Instant Pot makes them overly soft and mushy, which is key to creating an extra-smooth hummus. But what makes this hummus better than any other is the generous amount of tahini. It adds a nice sesame flavor and helps to achieve that highly desired creaminess. You can serve the hummus as is, with a drizzle of olive oil and a sprinkle of smoky paprika, or make my roasted pumpkin seed version (see Note) for something a little different. Just be sure to have fresh naan and/or pita chips nearby for scooping.

2 (14-ounce) cans chickpeas

2 garlic cloves, smashed

¼ teaspoon ground cumin

Juice of 1 lemon, plus more as needed

½ cup tahini

2 tablespoons extra-virgin olive oil, plus more for serving

Flaky sea salt

Toasted pine nuts, for serving (optional)

PRESSURE COOKER COOK TIME: 10 minutes, plus additional time to come to pressure

1. In the pressure cooker pot, combine the chickpeas, the liquid from the cans, and the garlic. Lock the lid in place and cook on high pressure for 10 minutes. Quick or natural release, then open when the pressure subsides.

2. Reserve ½ cup of the cooking liquid and drain the rest. Transfer the chickpeas and garlic to a food processor and pulse until mostly smooth, about 3 minutes. Add the cumin, lemon juice, tahini, and olive oil and pulse to combine, about 1 minute. While pureeing, slowly add the reserved cooking liquid, 1 tablespoon at a time, until your desired consistency is reached. Taste and add salt as needed.

3. Spoon the hummus into a bowl. Serve with olive oil and toasted pine nuts, if desired. Store the hummus refrigerated in an airtight container for up to 1 week.

STOVETOP COOK TIME: 30 minutes

1. In a large pot, combine the chickpeas, the liquid from the cans, and the garlic. Cover and cook over medium-high heat until the chickpeas are falling apart, 20 to 30 minutes.

2. Finish as directed for the pressure cooker.

To switch things up, I sometimes make this hummus with shelled and roasted pumpkin seeds (pepitas) in place of tahini. Pulse 1½ cups of toasted pepitas in the food processor until mostly smooth and they've turned into a paste, about 5 minutes. Add the pressure cooker chickpeas and follow the directions, using the pepita paste in place of the tahini.

MAPLE-CINNAMON ACORN SQUASH

SERVES: 4

PREP TIME: 10 minutes
COOK TIME: 45 minutes
TOTAL TIME: 55 minutes

My mom is much more of a baker than a cook, so when my brothers and I were young, it was mostly my dad who made dinner. That said, Mom had a few dishes in her repertoire, and one of them was roasted acorn squash with a dash of cinnamon and a good amount of butter. She'd make it every fall, and it's always been one of my favorite sweet-and-savory side dishes. The only change I made from Mom's recipe is to replace her brown sugar with maple syrup. It's a little less sweet and pairs really nicely with the cinnamon. As the squash roasts, the butter, maple, and cinnamon form a bit of a "sticky" sauce that puddles in the center of the squash. So good, it melts in your mouth. I like to serve this with a simple roasted chicken, as a holiday side dish, or even on its own.

2 acorn squashes, halved lengthwise and seeds removed

3 tablespoons pure maple syrup

1 teaspoon ground cinnamon

Kosher salt

4 tablespoons salted butter

1. Preheat the oven to 425°F. Line a rimmed baking sheet with parchment paper.

2. Place the squash cut side down on the prepared baking sheet. Bake until fork-tender, about 15 minutes. Remove from the oven and carefully flip each squash half. Drizzle the maple syrup over the squash and sprinkle evenly with the cinnamon and salt. Add a tablespoon of the butter to the center of each. Return the squash to the oven and bake until the squash is beginning to caramelize and brown, about 30 minutes more.

3. Remove from the oven and swirl the butter around the squash with a spoon to coat each half evenly. Serve warm.

A COCKTAIL FOR EVERY SEASON

When I started out, I didn't have a clue about how to mix a proper drink, but over the years I've learned a trick or two. As the majority of my family is now "of age," they've become fairly big on the cocktails. In an effort to keep up with them, crafting seasonal drinks has become a favored pastime of mine. With drinks, I can really let my creativity run wild and have fun mixing up fruity concoctions. These are my favorite seasonal cocktails. They're simple to mix, beautiful, and each one is deliciously refreshing. Bottoms up!

POMEGRANATE-THYME VODKA SPRITZ

SERVES: 4

PREP TIME: 10 minutes
COOK TIME: 5 minutes
TOTAL TIME: 15 minutes, plus chilling time

¼ cup honey

2 sprigs of fresh thyme, plus more for serving

1 (1-inch) piece of fresh ginger, peeled and sliced

8 ounces vodka

4 ounces elderflower liqueur, such as St-Germain

1⅓ cups pomegranate juice

Juice of 2 limes

3 to 4 (12-ounce) ginger beers

1. In a medium saucepan, combine the honey, thyme, ginger, and ½ cup of water over high heat. Bring to a boil and cook until the ginger is fragrant, about 5 minutes. Remove the pan from the heat and let the syrup cool to room temperature. Remove and discard the thyme and ginger.

2. In a large pitcher, combine the syrup, vodka, elderflower liqueur, pomegranate juice, and lime juice. Chill in the refrigerator until ready to serve, at least 1 hour.

3. Add the ginger beer to your taste just before serving and stir to combine.

4. Add ice to four glasses and pour the spritz over the top. Garnish each drink with fresh thyme.

SPICY STRAWBERRY PALOMA

SERVES: 1

PREP TIME: 10 minutes
TOTAL TIME: 10 minutes

1 tablespoon chili powder

1 tablespoon kosher salt

2 teaspoons granulated sugar

1 grapefruit wedge, for the rim and for serving

2 ounces silver tequila, such as Siete Leguas Añejo

Juice of ½ grapefruit

4 fresh strawberries, muddled

1 or 2 slices jalapeño pepper, seeded, plus more for serving

1 teaspoon honey, plus more to taste

Sparkling water, for topping

1. On a small plate, stir together the chili powder, salt, and sugar. Rub the rim of a highball glass with the grapefruit wedge and dip the rim in the mixture to coat.

2. In a cocktail shaker, combine the tequila, grapefruit juice, strawberries, jalapeño, honey, and ice. Shake well to combine. Strain into the prepared glass and top with sparkling water.

3. Serve with the grapefruit wedge and a slice of jalapeño.

The longer you shake your drink, the spicier it will become.

PEACH ROSÉ SANGRIA

SERVES: 6

PREP TIME: 10 minutes

TOTAL TIME: 10 minutes, plus chilling time

4 peaches, sliced

2 cups fresh or frozen raspberries

1 (1-inch) piece of fresh ginger, peeled and grated

1 bottle (750 ml) rosé wine, such as Pasqua 11 Minutes Rosé

4 ounces elderflower liqueur, such as St-Germain

Juice of 1 grapefruit (about ¼ cup)

Juice of 1 lime (about 2 tablespoons)

Sparkling water, for topping

Fresh mint or basil leaves, for serving

1. In a large pitcher, combine the peaches, raspberries, ginger, rosé, elderflower liqueur, grapefruit juice, and lime juice. Chill in the refrigerator until ready to serve.

2. Fill six glasses with ice and pour in the sangria. Top with sparkling water and garnish with the mint.

If you can't find fresh peaches, you can use frozen. Just allow an extra hour of sitting time for the peaches to thaw and sweeten the sangria. You can also make this drink with other fruits, such as berries, apples, or pears.

HONEYCRISP APPLE BOURBON SMASH

. . . .

SERVES: 1

. . . .

PREP TIME: 5 minutes   **TOTAL TIME:** 5 minutes

¼ cup apple cider

1 teaspoon orange zest

2 tablespoons orange juice

1 tablespoon apple butter

2 ounces bourbon

1 teaspoon balsamic vinegar (optional, but delicious)

Ginger beer, for topping

Honeycrisp apple slices, for garnish

1. In a cocktail shaker, combine the apple cider, orange zest, orange juice, apple butter, bourbon, and vinegar (if using). Shake well to combine.

2. Add ice to an old-fashioned glass and strain the bourbon smash over it. Top with ginger beer and garnish with apple slices.

SALAD &
SOUP

SUN-DRIED TOMATO AND AVOCADO SALAD

WITH CHICKEN

....

SERVES: 6

....

PREP TIME: 10 minutes
COOK TIME: 10 minutes
TOTAL TIME: 20 minutes

Sun-dried tomatoes packed in oil are one of my pantry staples. They are my go-to when I want to add major flavor, since they can take any recipe from just okay to delicious. Enter this salad: I make it often, for lunch or for dinner, and the oil-packed tomatoes are key. I like to use the oil left in the jar to make the salad vinaigrette—it's already seasoned with herbs and garlic, so it makes for an *extra*-flavorful dressing—and the oil the tomatoes soak up in the jar makes them plump, with a meaty texture and hearty taste. When I have some paprika-rubbed rotisserie chicken (see page 178) on hand, I shred it to add protein to the salad. I often leave the chicken out or replace it with pan-fried chickpeas for a vegetarian protein source.

SALAD

6 cups fresh spinach

2 avocados, sliced

1 to 2 cups shredded cooked chicken

½ cup sun-dried tomatoes packed in olive oil, drained and oil reserved

4 ounces crumbled feta cheese

⅓ cup toasted pine nuts

2 tablespoons roughly chopped fresh dill

BACON VINAIGRETTE

4 slices thick-cut bacon, chopped

2 garlic cloves, smashed

1 sprig of fresh rosemary

¼ cup reserved sun-dried tomato oil

Juice of ½ lemon

1 tablespoon apple cider vinegar

1 tablespoon honey

1 teaspoon Dijon mustard

Crushed red pepper flakes

Kosher salt and freshly ground pepper

1. **Make the salad.** In a large bowl, toss together the spinach, avocados, chicken, sun-dried tomatoes, feta, pine nuts, and dill. Set aside.

2. **Make the vinaigrette.** Heat a large skillet over medium-high heat. Add the bacon, garlic, and rosemary and cook, stirring frequently, until the bacon is crisp, its fat is rendered, and the rosemary is fried, 4 to 5 minutes. Remove and discard the garlic and rosemary. Drain off all but 1 tablespoon of the bacon fat. Add the reserved sun-dried tomato oil, lemon juice, vinegar, honey, mustard, and a pinch each of red pepper flakes, salt, and pepper. Stir to combine and cook until warmed through, about 1 minute.

3. Drizzle the warm vinaigrette over the salad and toss to coat. Serve immediately.

....

This is a great salad to layer into a jar for an on-the-go lunch. Follow this order: vinaigrette, shredded chicken, sun-dried tomatoes, spinach, feta, pine nuts, avocado. Squeeze lemon juice over the avocado to keep it from browning. Store refrigerated for up to 1 day. To eat, dump the salad out into a bowl, toss, sprinkle with dill, and enjoy!

EVERYTHING BAGEL SALAD

WITH WHITE BEANS AND PESTO

....
SERVES: 4
....

PREP TIME: 10 minutes
COOK TIME: 5 minutes
TOTAL TIME: 15 minutes

This is the salad I make when I'm low on fresh ingredients and have to rely mostly on pantry staples. It's beyond delicious and so easy, and it takes just minutes to throw together. Grab that bagel you have stashed away in the freezer for "emergencies" (don't we all have one?) and toast it up with a little olive oil until golden (aka it's time to pan-fry that 9-1-1 bagel). I bet you never thought you'd be eating it on the best fifteen-minute salad—one that's both healthy *and* satisfying. If the bagel isn't everything flavored, or even if it's a baguette, this salad will still be delicious, I promise!

3 tablespoons extra-virgin olive oil

1 everything bagel, roughly torn

1 (15-ounce) can cannellini beans, drained and rinsed

⅓ cup Lemon Basil Pesto (page 19) or store-bought pesto

1 tablespoon white wine vinegar

Juice of 1 lemon

Flaky sea salt

Crushed red pepper flakes

6 cups baby arugula

¼ cup freshly shaved Parmesan cheese

1 tablespoon Everything Bagel Spice (page 17) or store-bought blend

1. In a large skillet, heat 2 tablespoons of the olive oil over medium heat. When the oil shimmers, add the bagel and cook, tossing occasionally, until lightly toasted, about 5 minutes. Remove the pan from the heat and set aside.

2. In a medium bowl, toss together the cannellini beans, pesto, the remaining 1 tablespoon of olive oil, the vinegar, lemon juice, and a pinch each of flaky salt and red pepper flakes. Add the arugula, Parmesan, and everything bagel spice and toss to combine.

3. Divide the salad among four bowls and top with the bagel croutons.

MARINATED HEIRLOOM TOMATO AND NECTARINE SALAD

WITH GARDEN HERBS

SERVES: 6

PREP TIME: 15 minutes
TOTAL TIME: 15 minutes,
plus marinating time

I love a fruit-filled salad. In fact, most of my salads tend to be heavier on the fruit than the vegetables. Some people are immediately into this, while others need a little nudging. However, once they give it a try, there's no turning back. These are the best kind of salads in the summer months. Here I've combined some of summer's produce to make a salad that's both simple and delicious. Sweet nectarines add crunch, tiny cherry tomatoes add a burst of summertime with every bite, and marinating the fruits in an herb-filled vinaigrette infuses them with even more flavor. Of course, no salad is complete without cheese. And when using sweet stone fruits, burrata is my preferred cheese. Its rich creaminess balances out the sweetness perfectly.

¼ cup extra-virgin olive oil

3 tablespoons shelled, roasted pistachios

2 tablespoons balsamic vinegar or white balsamic vinegar

2 teaspoons honey

12 fresh basil leaves, roughly chopped

2 sprigs of fresh thyme, chopped

1 garlic clove, grated

Crushed red pepper flakes

Kosher salt

2½ cups cherry tomatoes, halved

2 nectarines, cut into wedges

2 balls of burrata cheese, roughly torn

2 tablespoons chopped fresh chives, for serving

Flaky sea salt, for serving

1. In a food processor, combine the olive oil, pistachios, vinegar, honey, basil, thyme, garlic, red pepper flakes, and a pinch of salt and pulse until finely ground, about 1 minute.

2. In a medium bowl, combine the tomatoes and nectarines. Add the pistachio puree, tossing to coat. Let marinate at room temperature for 10 to 20 minutes or covered with plastic wrap overnight in the fridge.

3. To serve, divide the salad evenly among six bowls and top each with some torn burrata, chives, and a pinch of flaky salt.

AUTUMN HARVEST SALAD

. . . .
SERVES: 6
. . . .

PREP TIME: 15 minutes
COOK TIME: 20 minutes
TOTAL TIME: 35 minutes

Every autumn I create a new harvest salad to celebrate the season, and this version is without a doubt my favorite. Persimmons are the most underrated autumn fruit. They have a sweet, honey-like flavor, and are great even on their own. Just beware: if they're not quite ripe, they'll make your mouth feel fuzzy! If you can't find persimmons or would like to switch up the fruit, Honeycrisp apples are the best replacement and are equally delicious. Serve this dish as a side salad for your next autumn dinner party or even on your Thanksgiving table. It's easy, festive, and delicious.

SALAD

1 cup raw pecans

1 tablespoon extra-virgin olive oil

3 tablespoons pure maple syrup

½ teaspoon ground cinnamon

Pinch of kosher salt

2 bunches of Tuscan kale, stemmed and shredded

3 Honeycrisp apples or Fuyu persimmons, thinly sliced

Seeds from 1 pomegranate

4 slices thick-cut bacon, chopped

½ cup crumbled or cubed blue cheese, goat cheese, or feta

CARAMELIZED SHALLOT AND CIDER VINAIGRETTE

⅓ cup extra-virgin olive oil

1 small shallot, thinly sliced

2 tablespoons apple cider vinegar

1 tablespoon apple butter

1 tablespoon fresh thyme leaves

Crushed red pepper flakes

Kosher salt and freshly ground pepper

1. Preheat the oven to 350°F. Line a baking sheet with parchment paper.

2. **Make the salad.** On the prepared baking sheet, toss together the pecans, olive oil, maple syrup, cinnamon, and salt. Arrange the pecans in a single layer. Bake until the pecans are toasted, 10 to 15 minutes.

3. Meanwhile, in a large salad bowl, toss together the kale, apples, and pomegranate seeds.

4. In a large skillet over medium heat, cook the bacon until crisp, about 5 minutes. Transfer to a paper towel–lined plate to drain. Wipe the skillet clean.

5. **Make the vinaigrette.** In the same skillet over medium-high heat, heat the olive oil. When the oil shimmers, add the shallots and cook until fragrant, 2 to 3 minutes. Remove the pan from the heat and let the shallots cool slightly. Add the vinegar, apple butter, thyme, red pepper flakes, salt, and pepper, and stir to combine and warm through, about 1 minute.

6. Pour the vinaigrette over the salad, tossing to combine. Top with the bacon, toasted pecans, and cheese, gently tossing to combine. Serve immediately.

GINGERED THAI STEAK AND PEPPER SALAD

SERVES: 4

PREP TIME: 20 minutes
COOK TIME: 20 minutes
TOTAL TIME: 40 minutes,
plus marinating time

As far as dinner salads go, this one has to be my family's favorite. The spicy, sweet, and tangy dish uses a mix of fresh vegetables, sautéed bell peppers, and pan-fried flank steak. It's colorful, healthy, and ready for eating in under an hour. The bulk of the flavor comes from the vinaigrette, made with toasted sesame oil, soy sauce, and ginger. You can make the vinaigrette over the weekend, as part of your meal prep, so all you have to do is cook the steak and toss together the salad when you're ready to eat. If nectarines are not in season, opt for fresh mango or pineapple chunks. Both are great options and add that perfect touch of sweetness.

GINGER-SOY VINAIGRETTE

2 tablespoons toasted sesame oil

2 tablespoons low-sodium soy sauce

1 tablespoon fish sauce

3 tablespoons honey

Juice of 2 limes

1 red Fresno or jalapeño pepper, seeded and chopped (optional)

1 (1-inch) piece of fresh ginger, peeled and grated

Kosher salt

THAI STEAK SALAD

½ pound hanger or flank steak

Freshly ground pepper

1 tablespoon unsalted butter

3 red bell peppers, seeded and thinly sliced

6 cups mixed greens, such as shredded cabbage and arugula

2 nectarines, thinly sliced

2 Persian cucumbers, sliced

¼ cup fresh Thai or regular basil, roughly torn

6 fresh mint leaves, roughly torn

1 avocado, sliced, for serving

2 tablespoons roasted peanuts, chopped, for serving

1. **Make the vinaigrette.** Combine the sesame oil, soy sauce, fish sauce, honey, lime juice, Fresno pepper (if using), ginger, and a pinch of salt in a small bowl or glass jar. Whisk or seal and shake to combine.

2. **Make the steak.** In a large bowl or zip-top bag, combine the steak with half of the vinaigrette and season with pepper. Massage the steak until completely coated and let marinate at room temperature for 10 minutes or up to overnight in the fridge.

3. Heat a large, heavy-bottomed skillet over high heat for about 2 minutes. Add the steak and sear on one side for 4 minutes and then flip and cook on the other side until medium-rare, about 3 minutes more. Add the butter to the pan and, once melted, spoon it over the steak and cook for 1 minute more. Remove the steak from the skillet and let it rest on a cutting board for about 10 minutes.

4. Add the peppers to the same skillet and cook, stirring occasionally, until they are just charred on the edges, 3 to 4 minutes. Remove the pan from the heat.

5. **Make the salad.** In a large bowl, toss together the greens, nectarines, cucumbers, basil, mint, cooked peppers, and the remaining vinaigrette. Thinly slice the steak against the grain and add it to the salad. Top with the avocado and peanuts and serve.

FRENCH ONION SOUP

PREP TIME: 15 minutes
COOK TIME: See specific device method

A cheesy bowl of French onion soup is one of life's greatest pleasures. Even people who claim not to enjoy onions still love it. In fact, I've served up many a bowl to family members who "hate" onions but *love* this soup. The one thing I dislike about French onion soup is standing over the stove for an hour tending to the onions, so I figured out a way to eliminate that tedious step by using the Crock-pot. Slow-cooking the onions for a few hours allows them to caramelize without having to stand by and continuously stir them. It's the easiest way to deliver a soup that's deep in flavor, thanks to the low and slow cooking time. If you'd like to speed the process up, you can also do this recipe in the Instant Pot in just under an hour. Either variation is delicious—just be sure never to skip the final step: the cheesy bread is my favorite part!

6 tablespoons salted butter

3 medium yellow onions, thinly sliced

2 medium shallots, thinly sliced

1 teaspoon honey or brown sugar

2 tablespoons fresh thyme leaves, plus more for garnish

1 tablespoon chopped fresh sage

2 tablespoons all-purpose flour

1 cup dry red wine, such as Cabernet Sauvignon

2 quarts low-sodium beef or vegetable broth

1 tablespoon Worcestershire sauce

2 bay leaves

Kosher salt and freshly ground pepper

6 slices French bread

1 cup shredded Gruyère cheese

SLOW COOKER COOK TIME: 6 to 11 hours

1. To the slow cooker pot, add the butter, onions, shallots, and honey and stir to combine. Cook on low until the onions are caramelized, stirring once or twice, 4 to 6 hours.

2. Add the thyme, sage, and flour and cook until lightly browned, about 2 minutes. Stir in the wine, broth, Worcestershire sauce, and bay leaves, and season with salt and pepper. Cover and cook 4 to 5 hours more on low, or 2 to 3 hours more on high. Remove and discard the bay leaves. Taste and add more salt and pepper as needed.

3. Preheat the broiler.

4. Divide the soup among six oven-safe bowls (see Note, page 90). Add a slice of bread to each and top evenly with cheese. Place the bowls on a baking sheet and broil until the cheese is bubbly and golden brown, 3 to 5 minutes. Top with thyme leaves.

PRESSURE COOKER COOK TIME: 35 minutes, plus additional time to come to pressure

1. In the pressure cooker pot, combine the butter, onions, shallots, and honey and stir to combine. Lock the lid in place and cook on manual for 20 minutes. Quick or natural release, then open when the pressure subsides.

2. Using the sauté function, stir in the thyme, sage, and flour and cook until golden brown, 5 minutes. Add the wine, broth, Worcestershire sauce, and bay leaves and season with salt and pepper. Lock the lid into place and cook on manual for 10 minutes more. Quick or natural release, then open when the pressure subsides. Remove and discard the bay leaves. Taste and add more salt and pepper as needed.

3. Finish as directed for the slow cooker.

recipe continues

If you don't have oven-safe bowls, place the bread on a parchment-lined baking sheet and top evenly with the cheese. Bake for 8 to 10 minutes at 350°F. Top the soup with the cheesy bread.

STOVETOP COOK TIME: 1 hour 10 minutes

Melt the butter in a large pot over medium-high heat. Add the onions, shallots, and honey and stir to combine. Cook, stirring frequently, until the onions are softened, deep golden in color, and caramelized, 25 to 30 minutes. Stir in the thyme, sage, and flour and cook until the raw flour taste is eliminated, 3 to 5 minutes. Add the wine, broth, Worcestershire sauce, and bay leaves and season with salt and pepper. Increase the heat to medium-high and return the soup to a simmer. Cook until the flavors have melded, 15 to 20 minutes. Remove and discard the bay leaves. Taste and add more salt and pepper as needed. Finish as directed for the slow cooker.

CREAMY CHICKEN GNOCCHI SOUP

SERVES: 6

PREP TIME: 15 minutes
COOK TIME: See specific device method

It's hard to one-up a classic, especially something as iconic as a bowl of chicken noodle soup. I won't go out and say this dish is better than a really good bowl of chicken noodle soup; it is a little different, but it's definitely just as delicious. Think about it this way: this soup has all the flavors and vegetables you love in chicken soup but uses a creamy Parmesan broth and soft, pillowy gnocchi. It's the coziest lunch or dinner, best enjoyed on a cold winter's day. I recommend using mini gnocchi, which are about half the size of traditional gnocchi. If you can't find mini gnocchi, don't stress, you can use regular as well.

2 boneless, skinless chicken breasts

1 small yellow onion, diced

6 carrots, chopped

5 cups low-sodium chicken broth

1 cup dry white wine, such as a pinot grigio or Sauvignon Blanc

2 tablespoons fresh thyme leaves, plus more for serving

2 bay leaves

1 teaspoon paprika

½ teaspoon crushed red pepper flakes

1 Parmesan rind

Kosher salt and freshly ground pepper

1 (16-ounce) box mini potato gnocchi

½ cup grated Parmesan cheese, plus more for serving

¾ cup whole milk or heavy cream

2 tablespoons extra-virgin olive oil

2 pounds mixed mushrooms, roughly torn

4 garlic cloves, smashed

4 tablespoons salted butter

Zest from 1 lemon

SLOW COOKER COOK TIME: 5 to 6 hours

1. In the slow cooker pot, combine the chicken, onion, carrots, broth, wine, 1 tablespoon of the thyme, the bay leaves, paprika, red pepper flakes, and Parmesan rind and season with salt and pepper. Cover and cook on low until the chicken is falling apart, 5 to 6 hours.

2. During the last 30 minutes of cooking, stir in the gnocchi, grated Parmesan, and milk. Remove and discard the bay leaves and Parmesan rind.

3. Remove the chicken and shred it using two forks. Stir the chicken back into the soup.

4. Heat the olive oil in a large skillet over high heat. When the oil shimmers, add the mushrooms and season with salt and pepper. Cook undisturbed until golden, 5 minutes, then stir and continue cooking until the mushrooms have caramelized, 3 to 5 minutes more. Reduce the heat to medium and add the garlic, butter, the remaining 1 tablespoon of thyme, and the lemon zest. Cook, stirring occasionally, until the garlic is caramelized and fragrant, 3 to 5 minutes. Mash the garlic with a fork and add the mushrooms, mashed garlic, and butter to the pot and stir to combine.

5. Divide the soup among six bowls and top with thyme and Parmesan.

recipe continues

PRESSURE COOKER COOK TIME: 10 minutes, plus additional time to come to pressure

1. In the pressure cooker pot, combine the chicken, onion, carrots, broth, wine, 1 tablespoon of the thyme, the bay leaves, paprika, red pepper flakes, and Parmesan rind and season with salt and pepper.

2. Lock the lid in place and cook on high pressure for 10 minutes. Quick or natural release, then open when the pressure subsides. Remove the chicken and shred it using two forks.

3. Using the sauté function, add the gnocchi, grated Parmesan, and milk to the pressure cooker pot, stirring occasionally. Cook until warmed through. Remove and discard the bay leaves and Parmesan rind. Stir the chicken back into the soup.

4. Finish as directed for the slow cooker.

STOVETOP COOK TIME: 45 minutes

1. Heat the olive oil in a large pot over high heat. When the oil shimmers, add the mushrooms and season with salt and pepper. Cook, undisturbed, until golden, about 5 minutes. Stir and continue cooking until the mushrooms have caramelized, 3 to 5 minutes more.

2. Reduce the heat to medium and add the garlic, butter, 1 tablespoon of the thyme, and the lemon zest. Cook, stirring occasionally, until the garlic is caramelized and fragrant, 3 to 5 minutes. Remove the garlic from the pot, mash with a fork, and add it back to the pot along with the chicken, onion, carrots, broth, wine, the remaining 1 tablespoon of thyme, the bay leaves, paprika, red pepper flakes, and Parmesan rind and season with salt and pepper. Increase the heat to high and bring to a boil, then reduce the heat to low, cover, and simmer until the chicken is cooked through, 20 to 25 minutes.

3. Remove the chicken and shred it using two forks.

4. Return the soup to a boil over high heat. Add the gnocchi, grated Parmesan, and milk. Cook, stirring occasionally until warmed through, about 5 minutes. Remove and discard the bay leaves and Parmesan rind. Stir the chicken back into the soup.

5. Serve as directed for the slow cooker.

BROCCOLI CHEDDAR SOUP

WITH SEASONED PRETZELS

SERVES: 6

PREP TIME: 15 minutes
COOK TIME: 30 minutes
TOTAL TIME: 45 minutes

There's probably nothing that reminds me of my childhood more than Panera's broccoli cheddar soup, which was served in a bread bowl bigger than my face. It will forever be one of my most loved soups, but these days I much prefer to make it at home . . . because homemade is always better. The good news is that this version comes together in no time and is simple and quick to prepare. I keep it fun with seasoned pretzel "croutons," which are truly one of my most addictive creations. This soup is nostalgia in a bowl.

¼ cup extra-virgin olive oil

1 medium yellow onion, diced

¼ cup all-purpose flour

2 cups whole milk

4 cups broccoli florets

2 bay leaves

¼ teaspoon freshly grated nutmeg

¼ teaspoon ground cayenne pepper

Kosher salt and freshly ground pepper

3 to 4 cups shredded sharp cheddar cheese, plus more for serving

2 tablespoons fresh thyme leaves, plus more for serving

Seasoned Pretzels (recipe follows)

1. In a large saucepan, heat the olive oil over medium heat. When the oil shimmers, add the onion and cook, stirring, until fragrant, about 5 minutes. Whisk in the flour and cook until golden, about 2 minutes, and then gradually whisk in 2 cups of water, then the milk. Stir in the broccoli, bay leaves, nutmeg, cayenne, salt, and pepper. Simmer until the broccoli is tender, about 15 minutes. Remove the pot from the heat and let the mixture cool slightly.

2. Remove and discard the bay leaves. Transfer the soup to a blender or use an immersion blender and pulse until combined but still chunky, about 1 minute.

3. Return the soup to the stove over low heat. Stir in the cheese and thyme and cook until the cheese has melted and the soup is creamy, 5 to 10 minutes.

4. Divide the soup among six bowls. Top each with more cheddar, fresh thyme, and seasoned pretzels.

<10

SEASONED PRETZELS

3 cups broken large pretzel rods

4 tablespoons salted butter, melted

1 tablespoon Worcestershire sauce

1 tablespoon Everything Bagel Spice (page 17) or store-bought blend

1 teaspoon freshly ground pepper

½ teaspoon smoked paprika

1. Preheat the oven to 325°F. Line a baking sheet with parchment.

2. In a large bowl, combine the pretzels, butter, Worcestershire sauce, everything bagel spice, pepper, and paprika. Toss well, making sure the pretzels are evenly coated.

3. Spread the pretzels in an even layer on the prepared baking sheet and bake until fragrant and toasted, about 20 minutes, turning them halfway through.

4. Store at room temperature in an airtight container for up to 3 days.

GOLDEN BUTTERNUT SQUASH SOUP

WITH CRISPY SAGE

. . . .

SERVES: 6

. . . .

PREP TIME: 15 minutes
COOK TIME: 40 minutes
TOTAL TIME: 55 minutes

A silky-smooth butternut squash soup recipe is one that everyone should have in their back pocket. This recipe is a personal favorite come fall, and my whole family looks forward to it, too. Slow-roasting the squash in the oven is a necessary step, as it allows the squash to caramelize and become sweet. I use a little cayenne to balance out that flavor, then blend the soup with creamy coconut milk for an indulgent texture that's still healthy. The crispy sage and toasted pumpkin seeds are the perfect finishing touches, adding flavor and texture to every bowl.

5 cups cubed, peeled butternut squash

1 shallot, chopped

2 tablespoons extra-virgin olive oil

2 tablespoons pure maple syrup

1 tablespoon chopped fresh sage, plus 6 whole fresh sage leaves for serving

½ teaspoon ground cayenne pepper

½ teaspoon ground cinnamon

Kosher salt and freshly ground pepper

1 (14-ounce) can full-fat unsweetened coconut milk, plus more for serving (optional)

4 tablespoons salted butter

1 cup raw pumpkin seeds (pepitas), for serving

Flaky sea salt

1. Preheat the oven to 400°F.

2. In a large Dutch oven or oven-safe stockpot, toss together the butternut squash, shallot, olive oil, maple syrup, chopped sage, cayenne, cinnamon, and a pinch each of salt and pepper. Roast until the squash is tender, 20 to 25 minutes. Let cool slightly.

3. Transfer the roasted veggies to a high-speed blender or food processor and add 3 cups of water. Puree until completely smooth, 1 to 2 minutes. Return the mixture to the Dutch oven and stir in the coconut milk and 2 tablespoons of the butter. Bring the soup to a simmer over medium heat and cook until warmed through, about 5 minutes. Thin the soup with more water as needed.

4. Melt the remaining 2 tablespoons of butter in a small skillet over medium-high heat. Add the whole sage leaves and cook until crisp, about 1 minute per side. Transfer the sage to a paper towel to drain and, to the same skillet, add the pumpkin seeds. Cook until toasted, about 3 minutes. Remove the pan from the heat and sprinkle the pumpkin seeds and sage with flaky salt.

5. Divide the soup among six bowls and drizzle with some additional coconut milk, if desired. Top with pumpkin seeds and crisp sage leaves and serve.

SALSA VERDE AND BROWN RICE

CHICKEN TORTILLA SOUP

SERVES: 6

PREP TIME: 10 minutes
COOK TIME: See specific device method

I *love* chicken tortilla soup. I've made more variations than you'd think possible, but this version is my favorite. It has two key ingredients that make for an extra-flavorful soup: red enchilada sauce and salsa verde. It might seem odd to mix these two ingredients together, but trust me, the result is an extremely flavorful soup with just the right amount of smokiness and heat. I use brown rice to keep my soup on the heartier (but still healthy) side. I love topping each bowl off with sweet mangoes, avocado, cilantro for freshness, and, of course, plenty of crushed tortilla chips.

1 medium yellow onion, diced

2 garlic cloves, minced or grated

1 pound boneless, skinless chicken breast

1 teaspoon kosher salt

Freshly ground pepper

3 cups red enchilada sauce

3 cups salsa verde

¾ cup uncooked brown rice

Juice of 1 lime

½ cup fresh cilantro, chopped, plus more for serving

FOR SERVING (OPTIONAL)

2 cups lightly crushed tortilla chips

1 mango, peeled and diced

1 avocado, sliced

1 cup shredded cheddar cheese

½ cup full-fat plain Greek yogurt

SLOW COOKER COOK TIME: 4 to 7 hours

1. In the slow cooker pot, layer the onion, garlic, chicken, salt, and a pinch of pepper. Pour over the enchilada sauce, salsa verde, and 3 cups of water. Stir in the brown rice. Cover and cook until the chicken is falling apart, 6 to 7 hours on low, or 4 to 6 hours on high.

2. Transfer the chicken to a plate. Let cool slightly and shred it using two forks.

3. Return the chicken to the slow cooker and stir in the lime juice and cilantro. Taste and season with salt as needed.

4. Divide the soup among six bowls. Top each with tortilla chips, mango, avocado, cheese, yogurt, and cilantro, if desired.

recipe continues

PRESSURE COOKER COOK TIME: 20 minutes, plus additional time to come to pressure

1. In the pressure cooker pot, layer the onion, garlic, chicken, salt, and a pinch of pepper. Pour over the enchilada sauce, salsa verde, and 3 cups of water. Stir in the brown rice. Lock the lid in place and cook on high pressure for 18 minutes. Quick or natural release, then open when the pressure subsides.

2. Transfer the chicken to a plate. Let cool slightly and shred it using two forks.

3. Return the chicken to the pressure cooker and stir in the lime juice and cilantro. Taste and season with salt as needed.

4. Finish as directed for the slow cooker.

STOVETOP COOK TIME: 1 hour

1. In a large pot, combine the onion, garlic, chicken, salt, and a pinch of pepper. Pour in the enchilada sauce, salsa verde, and 3 cups of water. Stir in the brown rice. Place the pot over high heat and bring to a boil, reduce the heat to medium-low, cover, and simmer, stirring occasionally, until the rice is cooked through and the chicken shreds easily, about 45 minutes. Remove the pot from the heat.

2. Transfer the chicken to a plate. Let cool slightly and shred it using two forks. Return the chicken to the pot and stir in the lime juice and cilantro. Taste and season with salt as needed.

3. Finish as directed for the slow cooker.

BUTTER-ROASTED TOMATO SOUP

WITH HONEY'D BRIE GRILLED CHEESE

. . . .
SERVES: 4
. . . .

PREP TIME: 10 minutes
COOK TIME: 20 minutes
TOTAL TIME: 30 minutes

There are a lot of tomato soup recipes out there, but I can almost guarantee that this one is the best. It calls for just six simple pantry ingredients, requires one pot, and is delicious. I know this is a cheesy thing to say, but this tomato soup will warm your soul and melt away your winter blues. My secret is to slow-roast the tomatoes along with onions. Then I blend the soup with pesto for the perfect amount of herby flavor. It's delicious on its own, but a side of grilled cheese is never a bad idea, right? Mine oozes with Brie and honey and, yes, it's just as tasty as it sounds.

TOMATO BASIL SOUP

1 (28-ounce) can whole peeled tomatoes, such as San Marzano or Pomi tomatoes

1 medium yellow onion, quartered

3 tablespoons salted butter

2 tablespoons fresh thyme leaves

Kosher salt and freshly ground pepper

1 cup whole milk, plus more as needed

3 to 6 tablespoons Lemon Basil Pesto (page 19) or store-bought pesto

GRILLED CHEESE

2 tablespoons salted butter, at room temperature

4 slices sourdough bread

4 ounces Brie cheese, sliced

Honey, for drizzling

1 tablespoon chopped fresh basil or thyme leaves, plus more for serving

1. Preheat the oven to 425°F.

2. **Make the soup.** In a large Dutch oven or oven-safe stockpot, combine the tomatoes, onion, butter, thyme, and a pinch each of salt and pepper. Roast until the onion is soft and fragrant, about 20 minutes. Let cool slightly.

3. Using a slotted spoon, transfer the roasted tomatoes and onion to a blender or food processor and add the milk. Blend until completely smooth, 1 to 2 minutes. Return the mixture to the Dutch oven and cook over medium heat to warm through, 2 to 3 minutes. Stir in 3 tablespoons of the pesto. Thin with more milk, if desired. Taste and add more pesto, salt, and pepper as needed.

4. **Meanwhile, make the grilled cheese.** Use 1 tablespoon of the butter to coat one side of each bread slice. On the non-buttered side of 2 slices, place the Brie, honey, and basil. Close up the halves to make sandwiches.

5. Melt the remaining 1 tablespoon of butter in a large skillet over medium-high heat. Add the sandwiches, one at a time, and cook until the bread is golden brown and the cheese has melted, 2 to 3 minutes per side.

6. Divide the soup among four bowls. Cut each grilled cheese in half and serve on the side.

CRISPY CHICKEN KHAO SOI NOODLE SOUP

SERVES: 4

PREP TIME: 10 minutes
COOK TIME: 20 minutes
TOTAL TIME: 30 minutes

My brother Brendan first introduced me to khao soi, the Thai version of chicken noodle soup, after returning from a trip to Thailand. It's traditionally made with homemade northern Thai curry paste, coconut milk, and hand-cut rice noodles, but I've simplified the recipe to use pantry staples like Thai red curry paste and store-bought egg noodles. It comes together quickly on the stove, and while it's not totally homemade, it still has incredible depth. Fish sauce is the key ingredient here, providing that traditional Thai flavor. Top off each bowl of soup with plenty of cilantro and fresh lime juice!

2 boneless, skin-on chicken breasts (about 1 pound)

Kosher salt and freshly ground pepper

2 tablespoons extra-virgin olive oil

¼ cup Thai red curry paste

2 large carrots, sliced

2 (14-ounce) cans full-fat unsweetened coconut milk

3 cups low-sodium chicken broth

3 tablespoons fish sauce

1 tablespoon honey

2 cups baby spinach or chopped baby bok choy

8 ounces egg noodles

Cilantro, sliced chiles, and limes, for garnish

1. Season the chicken all over with the salt and pepper.

2. Heat the olive oil in a large stockpot over high heat. When the oil shimmers, add the chicken, skin side down, and sear until golden and crisp, about 5 minutes. Flip the chicken, add the curry paste and carrots, and cook until fragrant, 1 to 2 minutes. Stir in the coconut milk, chicken broth, fish sauce, and honey. Cover and bring to a boil. Reduce the heat to medium-low, cover, and cook until the chicken is cooked through, about 15 minutes. Using two forks, shred the chicken directly in the pot. Stir the greens.

3. Meanwhile, bring a large pot of salted water to a boil over high heat. Cook the noodles according to the package directions, until al dente. Drain.

4. Divide the soup among four bowls and top each bowl with noodles, cilantro, chiles, and limes.

PIZZA & PASTA

THE MEANEST, GREENEST PIZZA

SERVES: 4

PREP TIME: 15 minutes
COOK TIME: 15 minutes
TOTAL TIME: 30 minutes

This pizza is essentially a salad with bread and cheese on the bottom. It's the pizza to have when you're trying to eat healthy but still craving pizza in your life. It also happens to be one of my favorites, with its lemon basil pesto base and sun-dried tomato, Tuscan kale, and goat cheese . . . *all* my favorite flavors. Just as the pizza comes out of the oven, I top it with a tangy sesame arugula salad that really complements the dish and puts the perfect finishing touch on it. Actually, the salad is even delicious on its own! Assuming you have all of the ingredients on hand (which I bet you do—and if you don't, I recommend stocking them), this pizza comes together in just minutes. It's a great option for busy weeknights and laid-back weekends alike.

2 tablespoons extra-virgin olive oil, plus more for greasing

½ pound No-Knead Bread and Pizza Dough (page 20) or store-bought pizza dough

⅓ cup Lemon Basil Pesto (page 19) or store-bought pesto

⅓ cup sun-dried tomatoes packed in olive oil, drained

2 ounces crumbled goat cheese

2 cups stemmed and shredded Tuscan kale

8 ounces fresh mozzarella, torn

1 tablespoon champagne or apple cider vinegar

Zest and juice of 1 lemon

1 teaspoon honey

Kosher salt and freshly ground pepper

Crushed red pepper flakes

4 cups baby arugula

2 tablespoons toasted sesame seeds

1. Preheat the oven to 450°F. Grease a baking sheet.

2. **Make the pizza.** On a lightly floured work surface, roll out the dough to a ¼-inch thickness. Carefully transfer the dough to the prepared baking sheet. Spread the pesto over the dough, leaving a 1-inch border, then layer on the sun-dried tomatoes, goat cheese, kale, and mozzarella. Bake until the crust is golden and the cheese has melted, 10 to 15 minutes.

3. **Make the salad.** Meanwhile, in a medium bowl, whisk together the 2 tablespoons of olive oil, vinegar, lemon zest, lemon juice, honey, and a pinch each of salt, pepper, and red pepper flakes. Add the arugula and sesame seeds and toss to coat.

4. When the pizza comes out of the oven, spread the salad on top. Slice and serve.

SWEET AND SPICY PINEAPPLE PIZZA

···········
SERVES: 4
···········

PREP TIME: 15 minutes
COOK TIME: 15 minutes
TOTAL TIME: 30 minutes

My best source of food inspiration is my family. They're constantly providing me with fresh ideas and recipes to re-create from all over the world. My brother Brendan has traveled everywhere under the sun, and his ideas are always the best. We share the same assertion that a little fruit tossed into a recipe is always a good idea. And we especially enjoy a good pineapple pizza! This particular pineapple pizza was inspired by one of Brendan's travels just south of the border into Mexico—he calls it the TJ Hooker pizza. With a spicy chipotle base, extra cheese, and pineapple on top, this pizza is both spicy and sweet—and a true *delight*!

Extra-virgin olive oil, for greasing

½ pound No-Knead Bread and Pizza Dough (page 20) or store-bought pizza dough

½ cup Chipotle Salsa (page 32) or store-bought spicy tomato sauce

¼ cup fresh cilantro or basil, chopped

1 cup shredded fontina cheese

1 cup fresh pineapple chunks

½ cup grated pecorino cheese

2 green onions, chopped

1 cup baby arugula

1. Preheat the oven to 450°F. Grease a baking sheet.

2. On a lightly floured work surface, roll out the dough to a ¼-inch thickness. Carefully transfer the dough to the prepared baking sheet. Spread the chipotle salsa over the dough, leaving a 1-inch border. Sprinkle on the cilantro, then the fontina. Layer the pineapple on top and finish with the pecorino.

3. Bake the pizza until the crust is golden and the cheese has melted, 10 to 15 minutes.

4. Top with the green onions and arugula. Slice and serve.

GARDEN BASIL PEPPERONI PIZZA

SERVES: 4

PREP TIME: 15 minutes
COOK TIME: 15 minutes
TOTAL TIME: 30 minutes

Just about the only foods we've ever had success growing in our garden are fresh herbs and cherry tomatoes. Okay, it's a greenhouse, but I love the idea of a garden. Living in the mountains, up at almost ten thousand feet, doesn't create the best environment for growing produce. But we do what we can in our little greenhouse, and this pizza celebrates that. It's quite possibly the simplest, but also one of the most delicious. The cherry tomatoes burst in the oven as they cook, adding a layer of texture and a pop of freshness with each bite. While I love making this pizza during the summer months, cherry tomatoes are available year-round, so it's great any time.

1 tablespoon extra-virgin olive oil, plus more for greasing

½ pound No-Knead Bread and Pizza Dough (page 20) or store-bought pizza dough

¾ cup canned crushed tomatoes, such as San Marzano or Pomi tomatoes

1 cup shredded mozzarella cheese

1 cup shredded provolone cheese

8 pieces of large, thinly sliced pepperoni

2 cups red and/or yellow cherry tomatoes

1 garlic clove, minced or grated

Kosher salt and freshly ground pepper

Crushed red pepper flakes

Fresh basil, for garnish

1. Preheat the oven to 450°F. Grease a baking sheet.

2. On a lightly floured work surface, roll out the dough to a ¼-inch thickness. Carefully transfer the dough to the prepared baking sheet. Spread the crushed tomatoes evenly over the dough, leaving a 1-inch border, then layer on the mozzarella and provolone. Scatter the pepperoni on top.

3. In a medium bowl, combine the 1 tablespoon of olive oil, cherry tomatoes, garlic, and a pinch each of salt, pepper, and red pepper flakes. Spoon the tomatoes evenly over the pizza. Bake until the crust is golden and the cheese has melted, 10 to 15 minutes.

4. Top with fresh basil leaves. Slice and serve.

HARVEST BUTTERNUT SQUASH AND APPLE PIZZA

SERVES: 4

PREP TIME: 15 minutes
COOK TIME: 15 minutes
TOTAL TIME: 30 minutes

If ever there was a pizza that screamed Half Baked Harvest, this would be the one. I'm what you might call "fall obsessed," and every year when autumn rolls around I become my happiest self, cooking and baking away in the kitchen. This pizza combines all of my favorite fall produce into one of my favorite things to cook and eat: pizza. Caramelized shallots, sweet Honeycrisp apples, butternut squash, savory sage, and salty, crispy prosciutto. I add a good amount of cheese, of course, because this is pizza and because cheese is delicious. So good, so easy, so HBH.

1 tablespoon extra-virgin olive oil, plus more for greasing

2 shallots, thinly sliced

½ pound No-Knead Bread and Pizza Dough (page 20) or store-bought pizza dough

2 tablespoons apple butter

1 Honeycrisp apple, thinly sliced

1 cup shredded mozzarella cheese

½ cup shredded sharp cheddar cheese

½ small butternut squash, shaved into ribbons using a vegetable peeler

8 fresh sage leaves

3 ounces thinly sliced prosciutto, torn

Kosher salt and freshly ground pepper

Crushed red pepper flakes

2 ounces blue cheese, crumbled (optional)

Honey, for drizzling

Fresh thyme leaves, for serving

1. Preheat the oven to 450°F. Grease a baking sheet.

2. Heat the 1 tablespoon of olive oil in a medium skillet over high heat. When the oil shimmers, add the shallots and cook until fragrant, 2 to 3 minutes. Remove the skillet from the heat.

3. On a lightly floured work surface, roll out the dough to a ¼-inch thickness. Carefully transfer the dough to the prepared baking sheet. Spread the apple butter over the dough, leaving a 1-inch border. Add the sautéed shallots and the apple slices. Layer on the mozzarella and cheddar, then top with the butternut squash, sage, and prosciutto. Season the pizza with a pinch each of salt, pepper, and red pepper flakes and sprinkle the blue cheese (if using) on top.

4. Bake until the crust is golden and the cheese has melted, 10 to 15 minutes. Drizzle with honey and sprinkle with thyme to finish. Slice and serve.

POTATO AND BURRATA PIZZA

SERVES: 4

PREP TIME: 15 minutes
COOK TIME: 15 minutes
TOTAL TIME: 30 minutes

For the longest time, I never understood why you would put potatoes on pizza. It just did not make sense to me. The whole carbs-on-carbs thing seemed weird . . . even unnecessary—and that's a lot coming from me. One day, I ran out of ingredients to top my pizza with, and I finally caved. I put thinly sliced potatoes on my cheese pizza and, as you can guess, I loved it. I mean there's nothing not to love. Especially when you add flavorful lemon basil pesto, everything bagel spice (the best seasoning you will ever put on your potatoes), and fresh burrata cheese. Perfection on so many levels.

Extra-virgin olive oil

½ pound No-Knead Bread and Pizza Dough (page 20) or store-bought pizza dough

⅓ cup Lemon Basil Pesto (page 19) or store-bought pesto

⅓ cup shredded white cheddar cheese

1 medium potato, very thinly sliced (see Note)

2 tablespoons Everything Bagel Spice (page 17) or store-bought blend

8 ounces burrata cheese, torn

Fresh basil leaves, for garnish

Fresh thyme leaves, for garnish

1. Preheat the oven to 450°F. Grease a baking sheet.

2. On a lightly floured work surface, roll out the dough to a ¼-inch thickness. Carefully transfer the dough to the prepared baking sheet. Spread the pesto evenly over the dough, leaving a 1-inch border. Layer on the cheddar cheese, then the sliced potato. Drizzle the pizza with olive oil and sprinkle with everything bagel spice. Bake until the crust is golden and the potatoes are crisp, 10 to 15 minutes.

3. Top the pizza with burrata, allowing it to warm through, about 5 minutes. Top with fresh basil and thyme and drizzle with olive oil. Slice and serve.

I recommend using a mandoline for the best results slicing the potato, but a very sharp knife and a steady hand will work, too.

THREE-CHEESE AND NECTARINE WHITE PIZZA

WITH BALSAMIC DRIZZLE

SERVES: 4

PREP TIME: 15 minutes
COOK TIME: 15 minutes
TOTAL TIME: 30 minutes

This is my "all things summer" pizza. I know the nectarines may throw you off, but trust me, fruit on pizza is good. Plus, the bold blue cheese balances the sweetness from the fruit. If you absolutely despise blue cheese, you can use crumbled goat cheese or feta instead—either will be delicious! The blackberries are completely optional, though I love how they give a scrumptious burst of flavor in every bite. If you're looking for a fun and easy summertime pizza that's also pretty (and, of course, mouthwateringly delicious), this is it.

2 tablespoons extra-virgin olive oil, plus more for greasing and drizzling

½ pound No-Knead Bread and Pizza Dough (page 20) or store-bought pizza dough

1 tablespoon chopped fresh chives

¼ cup lightly packed fresh basil leaves, chopped, plus more for garnish

1 garlic clove, grated

½ to 1 teaspoon crushed red pepper flakes

3 ounces crumbled blue cheese

1 cup shredded mozzarella or fontina cheese

½ cup grated Parmesan cheese

1 nectarine or peach, thinly sliced

Kosher salt and freshly ground pepper

6 blackberries (optional)

Balsamic vinegar, for drizzling

Honey, for drizzling

1. Preheat the oven to 450°F. Grease a baking sheet.

2. On a lightly floured work surface, roll out the dough to a ¼-inch thickness. Carefully transfer the dough to the prepared baking sheet. Spread the 2 tablespoons olive oil over the dough, leaving a 1-inch border, then sprinkle on the chopped chives and basil, garlic, and red pepper flakes. Add the blue cheese, mozzarella, and Parmesan. Layer the nectarines over the top and drizzle lightly with olive oil. Season with salt and pepper. Bake until the crust is golden and the cheese has melted, 10 to 15 minutes.

3. Top with slivered basil and blackberries, if desired, and drizzle with vinegar and honey. Slice and serve.

SPINACH AND THREE-CHEESE

STUFFED SHELLS

SERVES: 6 TO 8

PREP TIME: 20 minutes
COOK TIME: 50 minutes
TOTAL TIME: 1 hour 10 minutes

Homemade stuffed shells have become a family favorite. This recipe is not only delicious, it is also so fun to make and eat. Maybe it's the cheesy stuffed shells that remind me of cheese-filled ravioli but without all the work. Or the flavorful tomato sauce that's filled with roasted red peppers and spicy Italian sausage. Or maybe it's all that fresh mozzarella cheese on top? No matter the reason, this is a recipe I make whenever friends and family are in town. Everyone always enjoys it. I mean, what's not to love about cheese-stuffed pasta sitting in delicious tomato sauce? It's always good!

2 tablespoons extra-virgin olive oil

1 pound ground spicy Italian sausage

2 (28-ounce) cans crushed tomatoes, such as San Marzano or Pomi tomatoes

1 red bell pepper, seeded and sliced

2 teaspoons dried oregano

½ teaspoon crushed red pepper flakes, plus more as needed

Kosher salt and freshly ground pepper

1 (8-ounce) bag frozen chopped spinach, thawed and squeezed dry

1 (1-pound) box jumbo pasta shells

16 ounces whole-milk ricotta cheese

2 cups shredded Gouda cheese

1 cup fresh basil leaves, chopped, plus more for serving

8 ounces fresh mozzarella cheese, torn

1. Preheat the oven to 350°F.

2. Heat the olive oil in a large oven-safe skillet over medium-high heat. When the oil shimmers, add the sausage and cook, breaking it up with a wooden spoon, until browned, 5 to 8 minutes. Reduce the heat to low and add the crushed tomatoes, bell pepper, oregano, red pepper flakes, and a pinch each of salt and pepper. Simmer until the sauce thickens slightly, 10 to 15 minutes. Stir in the spinach. Taste and add more salt, pepper, and red pepper flakes.

3. Meanwhile, bring a large saucepan of salted water to a boil over high heat. Add the shells and cook according to the package directions, until al dente. Drain well.

4. In a medium bowl, combine the ricotta, Gouda, and basil. Transfer the mix to a gallon-size zip-top bag. Push the mixture into one corner of the bag, squeeze the air out of the top of the bag, and snip about ½ inch off that corner.

5. Working with one at a time, pipe about 1 tablespoon of the cheese mixture into each shell, then place them in the skillet. Sprinkle the shells evenly with mozzarella.

6. Transfer the skillet to the oven and bake until the cheese has melted and is lightly browning on top, 25 to 30 minutes. Let cool for 5 minutes, then top with fresh basil to serve. Store any leftovers refrigerated in an airtight container for up to 3 days.

....

If you're feeding a vegetarian crowd or just prefer to go meatless, you can omit the sausage and simply add more crushed red pepper flakes to taste.

ONE-POT CREAMED CORN BUCATINI

SERVES: 6

PREP TIME: 10 minutes
COOK TIME: 20 minutes
TOTAL TIME: 30 minutes

Not much beats out a *one-and-done* pasta recipe on a busy night. This bucatini is great for the summertime, when fresh corn and basil are readily available. My mom's always had a soft spot for both ingredients, so combining the two in a slightly spicy, buttery sauce seemed like the right thing to do. Stirring in a couple of tablespoons of crème fraîche toward the end of cooking creates the perfect creamy sauce that tastes incredibly indulgent. People will assume it took hours to cook, but in reality, it takes just about 30 minutes. You'll love it! For the best results, be sure to use a pot that's large enough to fit the bucatini pasta without having to break it up. Make sure all the pasta is submerged for even cooking.

4 tablespoons salted butter

4 ears yellow corn, kernels sliced from the cob

2 garlic cloves, minced or grated

2 tablespoons fresh thyme leaves

1 jalapeño or red Fresno pepper, seeded and thinly sliced

2 green onions, chopped

Kosher salt and freshly ground pepper

1 (1-pound box) bucatini

½ cup grated Parmesan cheese

2 tablespoons crème fraîche

¼ cup fresh basil leaves, roughly torn

1. Melt the butter in a large Dutch oven over medium heat. Add the corn, garlic, thyme, jalapeño, green onions, and a pinch each of salt and pepper. Cook, stirring occasionally, until the corn is golden and caramelizing on the edges, about 5 minutes.

2. Add 4½ cups of water, increase the heat to high, and bring to a boil. Add the pasta and season with salt. Cook, stirring often, until most of the liquid has been absorbed and the pasta is al dente, about 10 minutes.

3. Remove the pot from the heat and stir in the Parmesan, crème fraîche, and basil. If the sauce feels too thick, add a splash of water to thin it out. Serve immediately.

SPINACH AND ARTICHOKE

MAC-AND-CHEESE BAKE

SERVES: 6 TO 8

PREP TIME: 15 minutes
COOK TIME: 35 minutes
TOTAL TIME: 50 minutes

You know those fallback recipes? The ones you make over and over again? Well this is mine. It's the easiest and best mac-and-cheese recipe. It uses just one pot, and the ingredients and methods are simple. My trick is to first boil the pasta in *just* enough water to start the cooking process, then add milk and cream cheese. That means there's no boiling and draining the pasta and no fussing around with making a roux either. Plus the cream cheese creates a light and creamy sauce without having to add any additional flour like in a béchamel. What's really great about this recipe is just how adaptable it is. When my brothers are around, I omit the veggies, but I include a few chipotle peppers in adobo, and I use half pepper Jack and half cheddar cheese. It's one of their favorites!

6 tablespoons salted butter, at room temperature, plus more for greasing

1 (1-pound) box short-cut pasta, such as macaroni

2 cups whole milk (see Note)

1 (8-ounce) package cream cheese, cubed

3 cups shredded sharp cheddar cheese

Kosher salt and freshly ground pepper

Ground cayenne pepper

2 cups packed fresh baby spinach, chopped

1 (8-ounce) jar marinated artichokes, drained and roughly chopped

1½ cups crushed Ritz crackers (about 1 sleeve)

¾ teaspoon garlic powder

1. Preheat the oven to 375°F. Grease a 9 × 13-inch baking dish.

2. In a large saucepan, bring 4 cups of salted water to a boil over high heat. Add the pasta and cook, stirring occasionally, for 8 minutes. Stir in the milk and cream cheese and cook until the cream cheese has melted and the pasta is al dente, about 5 minutes more.

3. Remove the pan from the heat and stir in 2 cups of the cheddar and 3 tablespoons of the butter. Season with salt, pepper, and cayenne. Stir in the spinach and artichokes. If the sauce feels too thick, add ¼ cup of milk or water to thin it.

4. Transfer the mixture to the prepared baking dish. Top with the remaining 1 cup of cheddar.

5. In a medium bowl, stir together the crackers, the remaining 3 tablespoons of butter, and the garlic powder. Sprinkle the crumbs evenly over the mac and cheese.

6. Bake until the sauce is bubbling and the crumbs are golden, about 20 minutes. Let cool for 5 minutes and serve. Store any leftovers refrigerated in an airtight container for up to 3 days.

Have a little extra milk or water on hand. Once you've added everything, you can decide whether you're happy with the consistency. If you need to thin the sauce out a bit, simply add more liquid.

PENNE ALLA VODKA TWO WAYS

SERVES: 8

PREP TIME: 10 minutes
COOK TIME: 20 minutes
TOTAL TIME: about 30 minutes

Penne alla vodka might not have been a dish that I grew up eating—we were more buttered noodle people—but it's one I make all the time now. To keep my sauce extra flavorful, I like to use two varieties of tomatoes: chopped Italian and sun-dried. The sun-dried tomatoes add a more intense and slightly sweet tomato flavor that I find especially delicious and that helps to set this vodka sauce apart from others. In small amounts, the vodka boosts and intensifies the aroma of the sauce and adds a sharp bite that balances out some of the sweetness from the tomatoes. The key is the slow simmering, which releases its flavor and cooks out the alcohol—making this recipe super kid-friendly!

You can make this vodka sauce two ways. Go the traditional route and serve it over penne, or go the cheesier route and turn it into a pasta bake (method included here) perfect for making ahead. Either way is delicious.

4 tablespoons salted butter

2 garlic cloves, minced or grated

½ teaspoon crushed red pepper flakes

½ cup vodka

1 (28-ounce) can crushed tomatoes, such as San Marzano or Pomi tomatoes

½ cup sun-dried tomatoes packed in olive oil, drained and chopped

Kosher salt and freshly ground pepper

¾ cup heavy cream

1 (1-pound) box penne

1 cup grated Parmesan cheese, plus more for serving

Fresh basil, for serving

~ TO SERVE TRADITIONALLY ~

1. In a large saucepan, combine the butter, garlic, and red pepper flakes over medium-low heat. Cook, stirring often, until the butter is melted and the garlic is fragrant, about 5 minutes. Add the vodka and bring to a simmer. Cook until reduced by one-third, 2 to 3 minutes more. Add the crushed tomatoes, sun-dried tomatoes, and a large pinch each of salt and pepper. Simmer the sauce over medium heat until reduced slightly, 10 to 15 minutes. Transfer the sauce to a blender or use an immersion blender to puree the sauce until smooth, 1 minute. Stir in the cream until combined.

2. Meanwhile, bring a large saucepan of salted water to a boil over high heat. Add the penne and cook according to the package directions, until al dente. Drain and add the pasta and Parmesan to the sauce, tossing to combine.

3. To serve traditionally, divide the pasta among eight plates or bowls. Garnish with basil and Parmesan.

~ TO MAKE A PASTA BAKE ~

To make a pasta bake, continue through step 2 above. In a medium bowl, combine 16 ounces of whole-milk ricotta cheese with ½ cup of heavy cream. Transfer half of the pasta with sauce to a 9 × 13-inch baking dish, spoon the ricotta mixture over the pasta, then add the remaining pasta. Top with 8 ounces of torn mozzarella cheese. Bake at 425°F until the top is lightly browned, 30 to 40 minutes. Garnish with basil and Parmesan.

LEMON BASIL PASTA

WITH BALSAMIC BRUSSELS SPROUTS

. . . .

SERVES: 8

. . . .

PREP TIME: 15 minutes
COOK TIME: 15 minutes
TOTAL TIME: 30 minutes

If there is one thing I love, it's a good herby pasta that's flavorful, heavy on veggies, and fast cooking. Enter this lemony basil pasta with pan-roasted balsamic Brussels sprouts. It's hard to believe how quick and easy this recipe is, especially since it has so much going on. The key is to cook the prosciutto in the oven while boiling the pasta and sautéing the Brussels sprouts. By the time the prosciutto is crisp, the pasta will be al dente and the sprouts sweet and caramelized. Toss everything together with pesto, goat cheese, and a sprinkle of Manchego, and you'll have a super-tasty, texture-filled pasta dish. All ready in just about 30 minutes. *Bon appétit!*

1 (1-pound) box long-cut pasta, such as bucatini or fettuccine

4 ounces thinly sliced prosciutto, torn

3 tablespoons extra-virgin olive oil

1 pound Brussels sprouts, halved or quartered if large

Kosher salt and freshly ground pepper

2 tablespoons balsamic vinegar

1 jalapeño pepper, seeded and chopped

1 tablespoon fresh thyme leaves

1 cup Lemon Basil Pesto (page 19) or store-bought pesto

4 ounces goat cheese, crumbled

⅓ cup grated Manchego cheese

Zest and juice of 1 lemon

1. Preheat the oven to 375°F.

2. Bring a large pot of salted water to a boil over high heat. Add the pasta and cook according to the package directions until al dente. Reserve 1 cup of the pasta cooking water, then drain.

3. Meanwhile, arrange the prosciutto in an even layer on a parchment paper–lined baking sheet. Bake until crispy, 8 to 10 minutes.

4. While the pasta cooks and the prosciutto bakes, heat the olive oil in a large skillet over medium heat. When the oil shimmers, add the Brussels sprouts and cook, stirring occasionally, until golden brown, 8 to 10 minutes. Season with salt and pepper. Reduce the heat to medium-low and add the vinegar, jalapeño, and thyme and cook until the sprouts are glazed, 1 to 2 minutes more. Remove the skillet from the heat and add the drained pasta, the pesto, goat cheese, Manchego, lemon zest, and lemon juice. Add about ¼ cup of the pasta cooking water and stir to create a sauce. Add 1 tablespoon more at a time until your desired consistency is reached. Taste and add more salt and pepper as needed.

5. Divide the pasta evenly among eight bowls or plates and top each with crispy prosciutto.

GROWN-UP TOMATO-PARMESAN PASTA

SERVES: 2

PREP TIME: 5 minutes
COOK TIME: 20 minutes
TOTAL TIME: 25 minutes

Please raise your hand if you loved SpaghettiOs while growing up! My older brothers did, but by the time I came around, my mom had stopped buying them. However, when I came across anelli ("little rings" in Italian), I was inspired to create a homemade version of my brothers' old favorite. Though I can't say this recipe tastes just like SpaghettiOs, I *can* say with confidence that this pasta is delicious, super simple, and better than anything you could ever pour out of a can. I use garlic-infused olive oil to add depth to the sauce, a touch of tomato paste for just the right amount of tomato flavor, Parmesan cheese, and fresh basil. This dish is best for days when you need comfort food but you also need something fast and healthy . . . ish.

3 tablespoons extra-virgin olive oil

1 garlic clove, smashed

2 teaspoons chopped fresh rosemary

Crushed red pepper flakes

3 tablespoons tomato paste

¾ cup anelli, ditalini, or other short, tubular pasta

Kosher salt and freshly ground pepper

⅓ cup shaved Parmesan cheese

Fresh basil leaves, for garnish

1. In a medium saucepan, combine the olive oil and garlic over medium-low heat (see Note). Cook, stirring occasionally, until the garlic is fragrant, about 2 minutes. Add the rosemary and a pinch of red pepper flakes and cook until toasted and fragrant, about 1 minute more.

2. Remove the saucepan from the heat. Stir in the tomato paste, then add 2½ cups of water. Return the pan to high heat and bring to a boil. Add the pasta and season generously with salt. Cook, stirring often, until the pasta is al dente, about 12 minutes.

3. Remove the pan from the heat again and stir in the Parmesan. Taste and add more salt and pepper as needed.

4. Divide the pasta between two bowls and top with fresh basil. Serve immediately. Store any leftovers refrigerated in an airtight container for up to 3 days.

. . . .

It's important to keep the olive oil at a low temperature throughout step 1. If the oil is too hot when you add the rosemary and tomato paste, the rosemary will burn and the tomato paste will splatter.

PUMPKIN AND SAGE LASAGNA

WITH FONTINA

SERVES: 8 TO 10

PREP TIME: 30 minutes
COOK TIME: 55 minutes
TOTAL TIME: 1 hour 25 minutes

I'm often asked what my favorite dish to entertain with is, and my answer is always the same: lasagna. Whenever I'm hosting dinner for family and friends, more often than not there's a pretty large crowd. I've been cooking for big groups since I first started, so while my entertaining style isn't perfect, I've mastered a few recipes that are ideal for feeding the masses. Come fall and winter, I make this on repeat and serve it with my harvest salad alongside (page 84). This lasagna requires very little hands-on prep. My trick is to use no-boil lasagna noodles and layer them with a creamy pumpkin sauce filled with warming herbs and spices, like fresh sage and nutmeg. As the lasagna bakes, the noodles soften, the sauce thickens up to the perfect consistency, and all the cheeses melt together. It's the perfect cozy meal.

2 teaspoons extra-virgin olive oil, plus more for greasing

1 (14-ounce) can pumpkin puree

2 cups whole milk

2 teaspoons dried oregano

2 teaspoons dried basil

¼ teaspoon freshly grated nutmeg

¼ teaspoon crushed red pepper flakes

Kosher salt and freshly ground pepper

16 ounces whole-milk ricotta cheese

2 garlic cloves, grated

1 tablespoon chopped fresh sage leaves, plus 8 whole leaves

2 tablespoons chopped fresh parsley

1 (12-ounce) box no-boil lasagna noodles

1 (12-ounce) jar roasted red peppers, drained and chopped

3 cups shredded fontina cheese

1 cup grated Parmesan cheese

12 to 16 pieces of thinly sliced pepperoni (optional)

1. Preheat the oven to 375°F. Grease a 9 × 13-inch baking dish.

2. In a medium bowl, whisk together the pumpkin, milk, oregano, basil, nutmeg, red pepper flakes, and a pinch each of salt and pepper. In a separate medium bowl, combine the ricotta, garlic, chopped sage, and parsley and season with salt and pepper.

3. Spread a quarter of the pumpkin sauce (about 1 cup) in the bottom of the prepared baking dish. Add 3 or 4 lasagna sheets, breaking them as needed to fit. It is okay if the sheets do not fully cover the sauce. Layer on half of the ricotta mixture, half of the red peppers, then 1 cup of fontina. Add another quarter of the pumpkin sauce, and place 3 or 4 lasagna noodles on top. Layer on the remaining ricotta mixture, the remaining red peppers, 1 cup of fontina, and then another quarter of the pumpkin sauce. Add the remaining lasagna noodles and the remaining pumpkin sauce. Sprinkle the remaining 1 cup of fontina on top, then the Parmesan cheese. Top with the pepperoni (if using).

4. In a small bowl, toss the whole sage leaves in the 2 teaspoons olive oil. Arrange on top of the lasagna.

5. Cover the lasagna with foil and bake for 45 minutes. Increase the heat to 425°F, remove the foil, and bake until the cheese is bubbling, about 10 minutes more. Let the lasagna stand 10 minutes. Serve. Store any leftovers refrigerated in an airtight container for up to 3 days.

If you'd like to prepare this dish ahead of time, prep the lasagna through step 3 up to 2 days before serving, then cover it with foil and keep in the fridge. Allow it to sit at room temperature while the oven preheats, then pick up with step 4. Or, to make it up to 3 months before serving, cover the lasagna well with a layer of foil, then a layer of plastic wrap. Thaw the lasagna overnight in the fridge and bake as directed.

VEGETARIAN

BLACK PEPPER BUFFALO CAULIFLOWER BITES

SERVES: 6

PREP TIME: 20 minutes
COOK TIME: 35 minutes
TOTAL TIME: 55 minutes

I've always loved to experiment with cauliflower. Way back in the early days when I first started cooking, and even before I launched Half Baked Harvest, I would make buffalo cauliflower bites for family dinners. The rounded florets reminded me of a breaded chicken nugget, which is why I first thought to coat them in a spicy sauce. Nowadays, I make these black pepper buffalo cauliflower bites, which have a touch more kick to them. Before roasting, I toss the florets with a homemade buffalo sauce spiced with black pepper and smoky paprika, then I roll them in panko bread crumbs, Parmesan, and cheddar. These are definitely not your usual buffalo wing game-day fare, but in my opinion, they're so much better, especially with my quick-fix homemade ranch dip.

BUFFALO CAULIFLOWER BITES

½ cup extra-virgin olive oil

½ cup hot sauce, such as Frank's RedHot

2 teaspoons smoked paprika

1 to 2 teaspoons freshly ground pepper, plus more to taste

1 teaspoon garlic powder

Kosher salt

2 heads cauliflower, broken into florets (about 6 cups)

1¼ cups panko bread crumbs

½ cup grated Parmesan cheese

⅓ cup grated cheddar cheese

QUICK-FIX RANCH

½ cup full-fat plain Greek yogurt

¼ cup buttermilk, plus more as needed

1 tablespoon chopped fresh chives, plus more for garnish (optional)

1 tablespoon chopped fresh dill

Kosher salt and freshly ground pepper

1. Preheat the oven to 425°F. Line a rimmed baking sheet with parchment paper.

2. **Make the cauliflower.** In a medium bowl, combine the olive oil, hot sauce, paprika, pepper, garlic powder, and a pinch of salt.

3. In a large bowl, place the cauliflower and add half of the sauce, reserving the remaining sauce for another use. Toss to coat. In a shallow bowl, combine the bread crumbs and Parmesan.

4. Dredge the cauliflower in the bread crumbs, pressing to adhere. Place on the prepared baking sheet and repeat with the remaining cauliflower.

5. Roast until tender and golden, about 20 minutes. Remove the cauliflower from the oven and sprinkle the cheddar over the top. Return the baking sheet to the oven and continue roasting until the cauliflower is golden and the cheese begins to crisp, 10 to 15 minutes more.

6. **Meanwhile, make the ranch.** In a medium bowl, stir together the yogurt, buttermilk, chives, and dill and season with salt. Add 1 to 2 tablespoons of buttermilk to thin as needed. Taste and add more salt and pepper as needed. Garnish with chives, if desired.

7. Serve the warm cauliflower bites with the ranch alongside for dipping.

. . . .

If you love blue cheese as much as I do, I'd highly recommend crumbling a few tablespoons of a good, stinky blue into the ranch. It's delicious.

HOT-AND-SPICY POT STICKERS

WITH CHILI PEANUT OIL

MAKES: 18 TO 20 POT STICKERS

PREP TIME: 40 minutes
COOK TIME: 20 minutes
TOTAL TIME: 1 hour

My ideal Friday night is staying in and making pot stickers with friends. First of all, I'm a proud homebody through and through, so it's the perfect way to unwind after a busy week. Second, absolutely nothing beats a delicious homemade pot sticker, and these are my very favorite. I must admit that while this recipe is straightforward, these little dumplings do require some time to prepare. A mix of vegetables (I like cabbage, broccoli, mushrooms, and carrots), fresh garlic, and ginger is stuffed inside store-bought wonton wrappers and pan-fried in a little oil, yielding yummy pot stickers with crispy bottoms and soft sides. My trick is to coat the bottom of the pot stickers in raw sesame seeds before frying them. As they cook, the sesame seeds become perfectly toasted.

CHILI PEANUT OIL

½ cup sesame oil

1 garlic clove, smashed

2 tablespoons raw peanuts

1 tablespoon raw sesame seeds

1 to 2 tablespoons crushed red pepper flakes

1 teaspoon kosher salt

POT STICKERS

4 tablespoons sesame oil

1 (1-inch) piece of fresh ginger, peeled and grated

2 garlic cloves, grated

4 cups chopped mixed vegetables

2 tablespoons low-sodium soy sauce

2 tablespoons green onions, chopped

18 to 20 wonton wrappers

⅓ cup raw sesame seeds

1. **Make the chili oil.** In a small saucepan, combine the sesame oil, garlic, peanuts, and sesame seeds. Place over medium heat and cook, stirring, until fragrant, about 5 minutes. Remove the pan from the heat and stir in the red pepper flakes. Let cool slightly. Transfer the mixture to a food processor and pulse until the peanuts are finely ground, 30 seconds to 1 minute. Add salt and pulse again to combine.

2. **Make the filling.** Heat 1 tablespoon of the sesame oil in a large skillet over medium-high heat. When the oil shimmers, add the ginger, garlic, and vegetables and sauté, stirring until the veggies are cooked down, 5 to 10 minutes. Add the soy sauce and green onions and cook until all the liquid has evaporated, 2 to 3 minutes more. Remove the skillet from the heat and let cool.

3. **Assemble the pot stickers.** Lay the wonton wrappers out on a clean work surface. Working with one at a time, spoon 1 tablespoon of filling onto the center. Brush water around the edges, then fold the wrapper over the filling to create a half-moon, pinching the edges together to seal. Repeat with the remaining filling and wrappers.

4. Place the sesame seeds in a shallow bowl. Brush the bottoms of the pot stickers with water and then dredge them in the sesame seeds, pressing to adhere.

5. Wipe out the skillet used to make the filling and heat the remaining 3 tablespoons of sesame oil over medium heat. Working in batches, when the oil shimmers, add some pot stickers and cook until the bottoms are light golden brown, 2 to 3 minutes. Pour in ¼ cup of water and immediately cover the skillet with a tight-fitting lid. *Caution:* Stand back; the water will splatter! Reduce the heat to medium-low and steam the pot stickers until the wrappers are softened all over, 3 to 4 minutes. Repeat with the remaining pot stickers.

6. Let cool and serve with the chili oil alongside for dipping.

This chili peanut dipping oil may just be one of my favorite sauces—it's completely addicting. I like to make a big batch and keep it in my pantry to use for tossing together quick salads or topping Asian noodles. Stored in a glass jar in a cool place, the oil will keep for up to 1 month.

SPAGHETTI SQUASH ALFREDO

SERVES: 3 OR 4

PREP TIME: 15 minutes
COOK TIME: See specific device method

Spaghetti squash can be an intimidating ingredient to work with if you've never done so before, but don't let it stop you. It's a great pasta alternative that tastes delicious and can feel just as satisfying. My favorite (and the easiest) way to cook spaghetti squash is either in the Instant Pot or in the slow cooker. It may be surprising, but I cook the entire thing directly in there, right along with the Alfredo sauce. No boiling water, no turning on the oven, no mess on the stove. None of that! Just add all the ingredients and let your device do its thing. Once everything has cooked, just slice open the squash (which will be soft and a cinch to cut through), remove the seeds, scrape the stringy flesh out, and toss it back in with the sauce that, hooray, is already cooked! It does not get simpler.

If you are working with a larger squash, it may require an additional 5 to 10 minutes of cooking time when using a pressure cooker.

- 1 cup heavy cream
- 2 ounces cream cheese
- 6 tablespoons salted butter
- 2 garlic cloves, smashed
- 1 teaspoon dried parsley
- 1 teaspoon dried oregano
- ¼ teaspoon freshly ground nutmeg
- Kosher salt and freshly ground pepper
- 1 medium spaghetti squash (5 to 6 pounds)
- 1 cup whole milk
- 1½ cups grated Parmesan cheese
- ⅓ cup grated pecorino cheese

SLOW COOKER COOK TIME: 2 to 5 hours

1. In the slow cooker pot, combine the heavy cream, cream cheese, butter, garlic, parsley, oregano, nutmeg, and a pinch each of salt and pepper. Prick the squash all over with a fork and place it in the slow cooker. Cover and cook for 2 to 3 hours on high, or 4 to 5 hours on low. Remove the squash from the slow cooker and let it cool.

2. Meanwhile, to the slow cooker pot, add the milk, Parmesan, and pecorino and cook on high until the cheese is melted and the sauce is smooth, about 15 minutes. Remove and discard the garlic.

3. Cut the squash in half lengthwise, remove the seeds, and use a fork to scrape the spaghetti squash flesh into a large bowl; it will separate into strands. Return the squash to the slow cooker pot and toss it with the Alfredo sauce.

4. Divide evenly among three or four bowls and serve immediately.

5. Store any leftovers refrigerated in an airtight container for up to 3 days.

PRESSURE COOKER COOK TIME: 35 minutes, plus additional time to come to pressure

1. In the pressure cooker pot, combine the heavy cream, cream cheese, butter, garlic, parsley, oregano, nutmeg, and a pinch each of salt and pepper. Prick the squash all over with a fork and add it to the pressure cooker. Lock the lid in place and cook on high pressure for 15 minutes. Quick or natural release, then open when the pressure subsides. If the squash is still firm to the touch, cook on high pressure for 5 minutes more. Remove the squash from the pressure cooker and let it cool slightly.

2. Meanwhile, using the sauté function, stir in the milk, Parmesan, and pecorino and cook until the cheese has melted and the sauce has thickened slightly, about 5 minutes. For a thicker sauce, sauté 5 minutes more. Remove and discard the garlic.

3. Finish as directed for the slow cooker.

SPICY POBLANO TACOS

WITH FRIED SESAME HALLOUMI

SERVES: 4

PREP TIME: 15 minutes
COOK TIME: about 15 minutes
TOTAL TIME: 30 minutes

Tacos are something I will never tire of making . . . or eating. They're fun, fresh, and usually pretty simple to prepare. I often make these spicy poblano ones on taco nights, along with a bunch of different salsas and guacamole. These tacos are always the first thing on the table to disappear. Everyone, whether they are vegetarian or not, absolutely loves them. Poblano peppers add some smoke, while the jalapeños bring a subtle, spicy kick. To cool things down, I mix up a quick cilantro lime yogurt sauce, and finish off each taco with fried halloumi cheese. Yes, fried halloumi cheese. If you're unfamiliar with halloumi, it's a Greek cheese similar to feta that's excellent for grilling. It might seem odd, but go with me on this and fry up that cheese. It'll be the best thing ever to happen to your taco night.

TACO FILLING

3 tablespoons extra-virgin olive oil

1 medium yellow onion, diced

3 cups roughly chopped cauliflower

3 poblano peppers, sliced

2 garlic cloves, minced or grated

1 jalapeño pepper, seeded and chopped

3 tablespoons low-sodium soy sauce

¼ cup fresh cilantro, chopped

8 ounces cubed halloumi cheese

1 tablespoon raw sesame seeds

8 small flour or corn tortillas, warmed, for serving

1 avocado, sliced, for serving

YOGURT SAUCE

1 cup full-fat plain Greek yogurt

1 cup fresh cilantro

1 jalapeño pepper, seeded and sliced (optional)

Juice of 1 lime

Kosher salt

1. **Make the filling.** In a large skillet, heat 2 tablespoons of the olive oil over medium heat. When the oil shimmers, add the onion and cook, stirring often, until soft, about 5 minutes. Stir in the cauliflower and poblano peppers and cook until the cauliflower starts to brown, 5 to 10 minutes more. Add the garlic and jalapeño and cook until fragrant, about 1 minute more. Add the soy sauce and cook, stirring, until the soy sauce coats the vegetables, about 2 minutes more. Remove the skillet from the heat and stir in the chopped cilantro.

2. In a small skillet, heat the remaining 1 tablespoon of olive oil over medium heat. When the oil shimmers, add the halloumi and cook without moving it until golden, about 2 minutes per side, 4 to 5 minutes total. Remove the skillet from the heat and stir in the sesame seeds.

3. **Make the sauce.** In a blender or food processor, combine the yogurt, cilantro, jalapeño (if using), lime juice, and a large pinch of salt. Pulse until completely smooth, about 1 minute. Taste and add more salt as needed.

4. Add the filling to the tortillas and top with the halloumi, avocado, and yogurt sauce.

If you'd like to add more protein to these tacos, cooked lentils or beans are a great addition. Stir them in toward the end of cooking.

15-MINUTE
GARLIC-BUTTER RAMEN

....

SERVES: 2

....

PREP TIME: 5 minutes
COOK TIME: 10 minutes
TOTAL TIME: 15 minutes

As a kid who grew up in Cleveland, Ohio, I know all too well how brutal Midwest winters can be. Often, on extra-cold days I'd talk my mom into letting me stay home from school because I was "sick." She'd make a fire, bundle me up in blankets, and flick on the TV. They were some of the best days, and you know what made them even better? The bowls of Top Ramen and freshly popped popcorn that my mom would make for lunch. It was the ultimate comfort-food lunch. These days, my ideal bowl of ramen is salty, a little spicy, veggie filled, noodley, and generally just bursting with flavor. Nothing like the Top Ramen I ate so much of as a kid, but that's okay because my "adult" version takes maybe 10 minutes to make. We are ditching the broth and adding some butter, plenty of garlic, and tons of fresh basil. My suggestion? Take yourself back to the age of twelve, play hooky from work, make garlic-butter ramen noodles, and watch your favorite old-school TV shows all day long.

6 tablespoons salted butter

4 garlic cloves, minced or grated

1 (1-inch) piece of fresh ginger, peeled and grated

2 to 3 cups finely chopped, leafy dark greens, such as spinach or kale

2 packs of brown rice ramen noodles, seasoning packet discarded

3 tablespoons low-sodium soy sauce

¼ cup fresh basil, chopped, plus more for serving

2 fried eggs, for serving (optional)

Toasted sesame seeds, for serving (optional)

Freshly ground pepper

1. In a large skillet over medium heat, melt the butter, then add the garlic and ginger, stirring constantly. Cook until the garlic is fragrant and beginning to caramelize, 3 to 4 minutes. Add the greens and cook until wilted, 2 to 3 minutes more.

2. Meanwhile, cook the noodles according to package directions. Drain.

3. Add the noodles and soy sauce to the skillet, tossing with the garlic butter. Remove from the heat and add the basil, tossing to combine.

4. Divide the noodles between two bowls and top each with a fried egg, sesame seeds, and more basil, if desired. Season with pepper.

MUSHROOM "CHEESE-STEAKS"

SERVES: 4

PREP TIME: 10 minutes
COOK TIME: See specific device method

In the last few years I've really taken to mushrooms. They've become a vegetable I use in many dishes, often as a meat replacement or as an enhancement to sauces and soups. Here I've used a mix of mushrooms and peppers to create a vegetarian version that's just as melt-in-your-mouth good as its beefy counterpart. Mushrooms tend to have a "meaty" flavor and texture, so they're perfect here. The mix of peppers adds a bit of a Southwestern flair to the legendary Philadelphia sammie. And of course, no cheesesteak is complete without some melty, cheesy provolone. You can make these in either the slow cooker or the Instant Pot. Both ways will leave you with a sandwich that's saucy, messy in a good way, and truly crave-worthy.

2 tablespoons unsalted butter

1 large yellow onion, thinly sliced

1 tablespoon low-sodium soy sauce

4 portobello mushrooms, sliced

2 garlic cloves, finely chopped

2 poblano peppers, sliced

1 red bell pepper, sliced

1 tablespoon chopped fresh oregano

Kosher salt and freshly ground pepper

4 hoagie rolls, halved

4 slices provolone cheese

Yum Yum Sauce (page 214) or store-bought, such as Terry Ho's Yum Yum Sauce, for serving (optional)

SLOW COOKER COOK TIME: 2 to 4 hours

1. In the slow cooker pot, combine the butter, onion, and soy sauce. Add the mushrooms, garlic, poblano peppers, bell pepper, oregano, and a pinch each of salt and pepper. Cover and cook until the vegetables are tender, about 4 hours on low, 2 to 3 hours on high.

2. Preheat the oven to 400°F.

3. Divide the mushrooms and peppers among the hoagie rolls and then top with provolone cheese. Wrap each hoagie in a sheet of parchment paper, then in foil, and place directly on the oven rack until the cheese has melted, about 5 minutes. Serve immediately, with the yum yum sauce on the side, if desired.

PRESSURE COOKER COOK TIME: 15 minutes, plus additional time to come to pressure

1. In the pressure cooker pot, combine the butter, onion, and soy sauce. Lock the lid in place and cook on high pressure for 2 minutes. Quick or natural release, then open when the pressure subsides.

2. Add the mushrooms, garlic, poblano peppers, bell pepper, oregano, and a pinch each of salt and pepper. Lock the lid in place and cook on high pressure for 4 minutes. Quick or natural release, then open when the pressure subsides.

3. Finish as directed for the slow cooker.

STOVETOP COOK TIME: 25 minutes

1. Preheat the oven to 400°F.

2. Melt the butter in a large skillet set over medium-high heat. Add the onion and cook, stirring occasionally, until softened, about 5 minutes. Add the soy sauce, mushrooms, garlic, poblano peppers, and bell pepper. Cook, stirring occasionally, until the mushrooms are caramelized and the peppers are beginning to char, 5 to 10 minutes. Add the oregano and season with salt and pepper. Cook 1 minute more. Remove the skillet from the heat.

3. Finish as directed for the slow cooker.

FALAFEL BOWL

WITH AVOCADO AND LEMON TAHINI

SERVES: 6

PREP TIME: 20 minutes
COOK TIME: 10 minutes
TOTAL TIME: 30 minutes

If you've ever been to a Mediterranean-style restaurant, you're familiar with falafel, little fried balls traditionally made with a mixture of ground chickpeas and herbs. I use carrots and sesame seeds in mine as well. They're truly one of the most delicious little bites you will put into your mouth. Now, I know frying is not considered easy, but there's a trick with this recipe: Prepare and fry your falafel over the weekend or whenever you have a little more time to cook. Then pack the falafel and quinoa salad up in individual containers to enjoy for lunch all week long. The falafel holds up really well in the fridge and is just as delicious served at room temperature as it is right out of the frying oil. If you've never made falafel but you've been curious, this is the perfect recipe to try.

FALAFEL

1 cup chopped carrots

1 (14.5-ounce) can chickpeas, drained and rinsed

½ cup all-purpose flour

¼ cup raw sesame seeds

2 garlic cloves, grated

1 teaspoon ground cumin

Kosher salt and freshly ground pepper

Vegetable oil, for frying

QUINOA SALAD

½ cup fresh parsley, chopped

2 tablespoons chopped fresh dill or mint, plus more for serving

1 jalapeño pepper, seeded and chopped

Seeds from 1 pomegranate

Juice of 1 lemon

Kosher salt

2 cups cooked quinoa

1 avocado, sliced

2 Persian cucumbers, sliced

LEMON TAHINI

¼ cup salted tahini

Juice of ½ lemon

1 (1-inch) piece of fresh ginger, peeled and grated

1. **Make the falafel.** Add the carrots to a food processor and pulse until finely chopped, about 1 minute. Add the chickpeas, flour, sesame seeds, garlic, cumin, and a pinch each of salt and pepper. Pulse until the mixture is combined and a dough forms, 30 seconds to 1 minute. Using a spoon measure and your hands, roll the dough into teaspoon-size balls.

2. Clip a thermometer to the side of a large heavy-bottomed saucepan. Add about 1 inch of oil and heat it to 375°F. Working in batches, add the falafel balls and fry until golden and cooked through, 2 to 3 minutes. Using a spider or a slotted spoon, remove the balls from the saucepan and drain on a paper towel–lined plate.

3. **Make the quinoa salad.** In a large bowl, add the parsley, dill, jalapeño, pomegranate seeds, lemon juice, salt, quinoa, avocado, and cucumbers. Toss to combine.

4. **Make the lemon tahini.** In a small bowl, whisk together the tahini, lemon juice, and ginger until completely combined. Add water, a teaspoon at a time, to thin as necessary.

5. Divide the salad among six bowls. Top each with 3 or 4 falafel balls, drizzle lemon tahini over the top, and garnish with chopped dill before serving.

To use less oil when frying, form the falafel into flatter patties and cook them more the way you would pancakes. This method will only require about half the oil.

MOROCCAN CHICKPEA AND CARROT TAGINE

SERVES: 6

PREP TIME: 15 minutes
COOK TIME: See specific device method

Vegetables are a big part of Moroccan cooking, and whenever I'm making vegetarian soups and stews I tend to use a mix of Moroccan-inspired flavors. I make this tagine whenever I'm craving a detox or simply a good amount of spice, vegetables, and protein. You can prepare this whole recipe in the slow cooker or the pressure cooker, making it a great option any night of the week. Just throw everything in, set it, and come back to a colorful pot of warm vegetables, spices, and chickpeas. My favorite way to serve this is over steamed couscous with a side of warm naan.

1 medium sweet onion, finely chopped

1 (1-inch) piece of fresh ginger, peeled and grated

2 garlic cloves, minced or grated

4 carrots, chopped

1 red bell pepper, seeded and chopped

1 (14-ounce) can diced tomatoes

2 tablespoons harissa paste

2 teaspoons smoked paprika

¾ teaspoon ground cumin

¾ teaspoon ground cinnamon

Kosher salt and freshly ground pepper

Juice of ½ lemon

2 (14-ounce) cans chickpeas, drained and rinsed

½ cup fresh cilantro, chopped

Cooked couscous or naan, for serving

Seeds from 1 pomegranate (about 1 cup), for serving

Fresh mint, for serving

SLOW COOKER COOK TIME: 4 to 8 hours

1. In the slow cooker pot, combine the onion, ginger, garlic, carrots, bell pepper, tomatoes, harissa, 1 cup of water, the paprika, cumin, cinnamon, and a large pinch each of salt and pepper. Stir to combine. Cover and cook on low for 6 to 8 hours, or on high for 4 to 6 hours.

2. Just before serving, stir in the lemon juice, chickpeas, and cilantro and cook until the chickpeas are heated through, about 5 minutes. Add more water to thin the tagine as needed.

3. Serve over couscous or with naan and top with pomegranate seeds and mint.

4. Store any leftovers refrigerated in an airtight container for up to 3 days.

PRESSURE COOKER COOK TIME: 11 minutes, plus additional time to come to pressure

1. In the pressure cooker pot, combine the onion, ginger, garlic, carrots, bell pepper, tomatoes, harissa, 1 cup of water, the paprika, cumin, cinnamon, and a large pinch each of salt and pepper. Stir to combine.

2. Lock the lid in place and cook on high pressure for 6 minutes. Quick or natural release, then open when the pressure subsides.

3. Using the sauté function, stir in the lemon juice, chickpeas, and cilantro, and simmer on low until the chickpeas are heated through, about 5 minutes. Add more water to thin the tagine as needed.

4. Finish as directed for the slow cooker.

STOVETOP COOK TIME: 30 minutes

1. Heat 2 tablespoons of olive oil in a large pot set over medium-high heat. When the oil shimmers, add the onion, ginger, and garlic, and cook until fragrant, 3 to 5 minutes. Add the carrots and bell pepper and continue cooking 5 minutes more, until the carrots have softened. Add the tomatoes, harissa, 1 cup of water, the paprika, cumin, cinnamon, and a large pinch each of salt and pepper. Stir to combine. Cover and cook until the tagine has thickened and is the consistency of stew, 15 to 20 minutes.

2. Just before serving, stir in the lemon juice, chickpeas, and cilantro and cook until the chickpeas are heated through, about 5 minutes more. Add more water to thin the tagine, as needed.

3. Finish as directed for the slow cooker.

VEGGIE-LOADED PAD SEE EW

SERVES: 4

PREP TIME: 10 minutes
COOK TIME: 10 minutes
TOTAL TIME: 20 minutes

Living in a small mountain town in Colorado means our takeout options are limited. Consequently, one of my favorite things to do is create homemade versions of Asian takeout meals. Surprisingly, it's just as quick to prepare at home as it is to order out—not to mention healthier—since where we live, delivery times can honestly be hours! This veggie-loaded pad see ew is a mix of rice noodles, tangy soy sauce, vegetables, and scrambled eggs. It's kind of like fried rice, but much saucier, which I love. You can use a mix of your favorite vegetables, or even buy a pre-cut stir-fry vegetable mix to save on time and prep. Once you give this recipe a try you'll be glad you didn't order in!

8 ounces rice noodles

⅓ cup low-sodium soy sauce

1 tablespoon fish sauce

1 tablespoon oyster sauce

1 tablespoon honey

2 tablespoons peanut oil

2 garlic cloves, minced or grated

4 cups mixed vegetables, such as Chinese broccoli, bell peppers, carrots, broccolini, cauliflower, snow peas

1 jalapeño pepper, seeded and chopped (optional)

2 large eggs, beaten

2 chopped green onions or 1 tablespoon chopped cilantro, for serving

1. Bring a large saucepan of water to a boil over high heat. Add the rice noodles and cook, according to the package directions, until softened. Drain and set aside.

2. Meanwhile, in a small bowl, whisk together the soy sauce, fish sauce, oyster sauce, honey, and ¼ cup of water.

3. Heat the oil in a large skillet over medium-high heat. When the oil shimmers, add the garlic, veggies, and jalapeño (if using) and cook until the veggies are soft, about 5 minutes. Push the veggies to one side of the pan. Add the eggs to the empty side of the pan and cook, gently scrambling them, until they are just cooked through, about 2 minutes. Add the noodles and soy sauce mixture to the skillet and gently toss to combine all the ingredients. Simmer the pad see ew for 5 minutes, or until the sauce coats the noodles.

4. Top with green onions and serve immediately.

. . . .

If you find your vegetables are a little crisper than you'd like after cooking, simply cover the skillet and cook for a few minutes more. Doing so will steam the veggies and help get them to the crunch level you'd like.

CURRIED THAI SPRING ROLL LETTUCE WRAPS

SERVES: 4

PREP TIME: 20 minutes
COOK TIME: 10 minutes
TOTAL TIME: 30 minutes

As wraps go, these spring rolls are about as fresh and flavorful as it gets. Think of your favorite vegetable-filled version, but replace the rice paper wraps with vibrant butter lettuce. Now add curried peanut sauce and plenty of fresh herbs—and here you are! These make a great quick and healthy meal. You can even prepare the "filling" the night before to make a delicious grab-n-go lunch. I also love the peanut sauce spooned on top of salads, tossed with Asian-style noodles, or used as a dip for vegetables—I'd make some extra if I were you!

8 ounces rice noodles

2 red or orange bell peppers, seeded and chopped

2 carrots, shredded

1 cucumber, chopped

¼ cup fresh basil leaves, chopped

¼ cup Peanut Sauce (recipe follows)

8 large butter or romaine lettuce leaves

1 avocado, sliced

Chopped toasted peanuts, for serving

Chopped red Fresno chiles, for serving

Lime wedges, for serving

Thai sweet chili sauce, for serving (optional)

1. Bring a large saucepan of water to a boil over high heat. Add the rice noodles and cook according to the package directions, until softened. Drain and let cool, about 5 minutes.

2. In a medium bowl, toss together the rice noodles, bell peppers, carrots, cucumber, basil, and peanut sauce to coat. Divide the noodles evenly into eight portions and place each portion on a lettuce leaf. Top each with avocado, peanuts, chiles, and a squeeze of lime juice.

3. Serve with chili sauce alongside for dipping, if desired.

<10

PEANUT SAUCE

½ cup peanut butter

½ cup low-sodium soy sauce

2 tablespoons red curry paste

¼ cup rice vinegar

2 tablespoons sesame oil

In a blender or food processor, combine the peanut butter, soy sauce, curry paste, rice vinegar, sesame oil, and 2 tablespoons of water. Pulse until combined and creamy, about 1 minute. Add water to thin as needed. Store the sauce refrigerated in an airtight container for up to 1 week.

SPICY POTATO SHAKSHUKA

···········

SERVES: 4

···········

PREP TIME: 10 minutes
COOK TIME: 20 minutes
TOTAL TIME: 30 minutes

I love a good breakfast for dinner. In fact, my mom and I have been known to enjoy a stack of pancakes together at the oddest of hours. That said, I love a savory egg dish just as much, and this shakshuka recipe is a staple at any time of day, whether it's early morning or late at night. Shakshuka, an Israeli dish of eggs simmered in tomato sauce, is commonly made with chile peppers, onions, and spices. Of course, being the carb lover that I am, I've always felt the traditional dish was missing something . . . so I added potatoes. I find the potatoes really round out the dish, while still keeping it light enough for Sunday brunch but hearty enough for Monday night dinner. If you're craving more greens in your shakshuka, try adding a handful of baby spinach or kale to the tomato sauce.

2 tablespoons extra-virgin olive oil

1 medium yellow onion, chopped

1 pound baby Yukon gold potatoes, halved

2 teaspoons chipotle chile powder

1 teaspoon smoked paprika

Kosher salt and freshly ground pepper

1 (28-ounce) can crushed tomatoes, such as San Marzano or Pomi tomatoes

1 (12-ounce) jar roasted red peppers, drained and chopped

½ cup shredded sharp cheddar cheese

4 to 6 large eggs

¼ cup fresh parsley, roughly chopped, for garnish

2 tablespoons toasted sesame seeds, for garnish

4 slices crusty bread, for serving (optional)

1. Heat the olive oil in a large skillet over medium heat. When the oil shimmers, add the onion and potatoes and cook until softened, 8 to 10 minutes. Stir in the chipotle chile powder, paprika, and a pinch each of salt and pepper and cook until the onion is coated, about 1 minute more.

2. Add the tomatoes, red peppers, and ⅓ cup of water. Increase the heat to medium-high and bring the sauce to a low boil. Reduce the heat to medium and simmer until the sauce has thickened slightly and the potatoes are fork-tender, about 5 minutes. Taste and add more salt and pepper as needed.

3. Using the back of a spoon, create 4 to 6 evenly spaced wells for the eggs. Sprinkle the cheese evenly into each well, then carefully crack 1 egg into each, keeping the yolks intact (see Note). Cover the skillet and cook until the egg whites are set, 10 to 12 minutes.

4. Serve family-style topped with parsley and sesame seeds and with crusty bread alongside, if desired.

·······

It's important to wait to add the eggs until the potatoes are fully cooked. If you add the eggs to the sauce before the potatoes are tender, the eggs will be done cooking before the potatoes are cooked through.

CAESAR BROCCOLI

WITH EGGY FRIED TOAST

SERVES: 4

PREP TIME: 15 minutes
COOK TIME: 10 minutes
TOTAL TIME: 25 minutes,
plus resting time

My one and only experience with a true Caesar salad was when I was twelve. I was out to lunch with my mom's mom, my Nonnie, and ordered the Caesar salad—I was that very weird kid who actually loved salads. I remember enjoying it, but as soon as we got back to the car, I felt queasy. And, well, you can guess what happened next. Ever since that day, I've never ordered another Caesar salad. But I think you'll find that my alternative—a mix of finely chopped broccoli and shredded kale tossed with a lemony tahini and Parmesan dressing— is just as creamy and delicious as the original. To bulk up the salad, I serve it with some toast fried in olive oil, and an over-easy egg.

½ cup plus 3 tablespoons extra-virgin olive oil

Juice of 1 lemon

2 tablespoons tahini

2 teaspoons Dijon mustard

1 garlic clove, grated

¼ cup grated Parmesan cheese, plus more for serving

Kosher salt and freshly ground pepper

Crushed red pepper flakes

3 heads of broccoli, cut into florets and roughly chopped

1 bunch of Tuscan kale, stemmed and shredded

4 slices thick-cut sourdough bread

Flaky sea salt

4 fried eggs

1 avocado, sliced

1. In a large bowl, whisk together the ½ cup of olive oil plus the lemon juice, tahini, mustard, garlic, and 2 tablespoons of water until smooth. Add the Parmesan and a pinch each of salt, pepper, and red pepper flakes.

2. Add the broccoli and kale to the bowl and, using your hands, massage the dressing into the greens until the kale softens, 1 to 2 minutes. Let the salad sit at room temperature for at least 10 minutes or refrigerate for up to 2 days.

3. Heat the remaining 3 tablespoons of olive oil in a medium skillet over medium heat. When the oil shimmers, add 2 pieces of bread at a time and cook until golden, 2 to 3 minutes per side. Remove and sprinkle with flaky salt. Repeat with the remaining bread.

4. To serve, divide the salad evenly among four plates and top with a piece of fried toast, a fried egg, and avocado slices.

. . . .

If you like a lot of dressing or are working with large heads of broccoli, I recommend doubling up on the dressing. Store any leftovers refrigerated in an airtight container for up to 1 week.

SAUCY COCONUT AND CHICKPEA CURRY

SERVES: 4

PREP TIME: 15 minutes
COOK TIME: about 20 minutes
TOTAL TIME: 35 minutes

Extra-saucy curries are something everyone should know how to make. Not only are they healthy, they're also quick and easy to put together and mostly use stuff you probably have in your pantry. I want you to think of this recipe as more of a curry base of chickpeas, spices, curry paste, and coconut milk. I encourage you to get creative and add your favorite vegetables. During the fall and winter months, broccoli is my go-to. In the spring, I might use a mix of asparagus and green peas. And in the summer, fresh zucchini and sweet corn are both unexpected and delicious in this curry. There's a ton of room to play with in this recipe, so have fun and adapt it to your own personal taste.

8 ounces vermicelli noodles

4 tablespoons extra-virgin olive oil

2 (14-ounce) cans chickpeas, drained and rinsed

1 tablespoon yellow curry powder

1 medium sweet onion, diced

Kosher salt and freshly ground pepper

2 garlic cloves, minced or grated

1 (1-inch) piece of fresh ginger, peeled and grated

¼ cup Thai red curry paste

2 (14-ounce) cans full-fat unsweetened coconut milk

2 teaspoons honey

1 medium head of broccoli, broken into florets

Zest and juice of 1 lime

¼ cup fresh cilantro, roughly chopped

¼ cup fresh basil leaves, roughly chopped

2 ounces crumbled goat cheese

1 jalapeño pepper, seeded and sliced, for serving

2 green onions, sliced, for serving

1. Cook the noodles according to the package directions. Drain and set aside.

2. Heat a large saucepan over medium-high heat. Add 2 tablespoons of the olive oil, the chickpeas, curry powder, onion, and a pinch each of salt and pepper. Cook, stirring often, until the chickpeas are crisp, about 5 minutes. Add the remaining 2 tablespoons of olive oil and the garlic and ginger. Cook until fragrant, about 3 minutes more. Stir in the curry paste and cook until fragrant, about 1 minute more.

3. Add the coconut milk, honey, broccoli, and 1 cup of water and stir to combine. Bring the curry to a boil and cook until the sauce thickens slightly, about 10 minutes. Remove the pan from the heat and stir in the lime zest, lime juice, cilantro, and basil.

4. Divide the noodles among four bowls. Ladle the curry over the top of the noodles, sprinkle with goat cheese and top with the jalapeño and green onions.

5. Store any leftovers refrigerated in an airtight container for up to 3 days.

If you are reheating leftovers for lunch or dinner the following day, it might be necessary to add a little water to thin the curry, as it tends to thicken slightly once it hits the fridge.

ONE-POT

HERBY BUTTERED MUSHROOMS AND WILD RICE

SERVES: 6

PREP TIME: 10 minutes
COOK TIME: 50 minutes
TOTAL TIME: 1 hour

My favorite recipes tend to be the ones I've thrown together using whatever I have on hand in my pantry. That is how this recipe came to be, and it's one I now make once or twice a month. The key to this dish is to first cook the mushrooms in a little olive oil, which gives them a head start and allows them to brown on the edges before you add the butter, herbs, and rice. Once the rice and water are in, the mushrooms will infuse the dish with that umami flavor. To finish it off, I like to add cannellini beans, a sprinkle of fresh herbs, and shaved Manchego cheese. I promise you'll be making this one over and over again on purpose, too.

2 tablespoons extra-virgin olive oil

1 pound mixed wild mushrooms

Kosher salt and freshly ground pepper

6 tablespoons salted butter

2 shallots, thinly sliced

½ cup fresh basil leaves, roughly chopped

2 tablespoons fresh thyme leaves

1 tablespoon chopped fresh sage leaves

½ cup dry white wine, such as pinot grigio or Sauvignon Blanc

1¼ cups uncooked wild rice blend

1 (14-ounce) can cannellini beans, drained and rinsed

Juice of 1 lemon

¼ cup shaved Manchego cheese

1. Heat the oil in a large skillet over high heat. When the oil shimmers, add the mushrooms and season with salt and pepper. Cook, undisturbed, until softened, about 5 minutes, then stir and continue cooking until the mushrooms are caramelized, 3 to 5 minutes more. Reduce the heat to medium and add the butter, shallots, half of the basil, plus the thyme and sage. Cook, stirring occasionally, until the shallots are caramelized and fragrant, about 5 minutes.

2. Pour in 2 cups of water and the wine and bring to a boil over high heat. Stir in the rice, cover, and reduce the heat to low. Simmer until the rice is cooked and most of the liquid has evaporated, 40 to 55 minutes. Add up to ½ cup of water more as needed throughout cooking. Remove the pan from the heat and stir in the beans, lemon juice, and the remaining basil.

3. Divide among six bowls and top with Manchego to serve.

POULTRY &
PORK

WALNUT-CRUSTED CHICKEN

WITH HONEY AND BRIE

SERVES: 4

PREP TIME: 20 minutes
COOK TIME: 25 minutes
TOTAL TIME: 45 minutes

For whatever reason, I've found that most people only think to use Brie when the holidays roll around. This makes zero sense to me. Brie is one of the most delicious cheeses, and it can be used in so many different ways beyond the tried-and-true baked wheel that everyone serves at parties. It's time to broaden your Brie horizons. This chicken is crusted in walnuts, baked until golden, topped with Brie, and drizzled with honey. It's every bit as delicious as you can imagine—and it's the perfect way to enjoy Brie outside the holiday season without feeling an ounce of guilt . . . because chicken and walnuts are healthy foods. Balance, people, balance.

Cooking spray, for greasing

1 pound boneless, skinless chicken tenders

½ cup buttermilk

1½ cups finely chopped raw walnuts

2 tablespoons whole-wheat flour

1 tablespoon chopped fresh thyme leaves

½ teaspoon ground cayenne pepper

Kosher salt and freshly ground pepper

Extra-virgin olive oil, for brushing

⅓ cup honey

1 tablespoon Dijon mustard

4 ounces Brie cheese, cut into small wedges

1. Preheat the oven to 375°F. Lightly grease a rimmed baking sheet with cooking spray or oil.

2. In a large, shallow bowl, combine the chicken and buttermilk. Toss to coat.

3. In a separate large, shallow bowl, combine the walnuts, flour, thyme, cayenne, and a pinch each of salt and pepper.

4. Working with one piece at a time, dredge the chicken through the walnut mixture, pressing gently to adhere. Place the coated chicken on the prepared baking sheet as you work. Brush or drizzle the chicken with olive oil and bake until the chicken is cooked through, 15 to 20 minutes.

5. Meanwhile, make the honey sauce. Combine the honey and the mustard in a small saucepan over medium heat and cook until the honey is warm and pourable, about 2 minutes.

6. Remove the chicken from the oven and drizzle with half of the honey sauce. Top each tender with a wedge of Brie and bake until the cheese has melted, 3 to 5 minutes more.

7. Serve the chicken drizzled with the remaining honey sauce.

RED'S FAVORITE SCHNITZEL

SERVES: 4

PREP TIME: 10 minutes
COOK TIME: 20 minutes
TOTAL TIME: 30 minutes

At not even twenty years old, my brother Red has traveled to more places than most will see in a lifetime. His snowboarding has taken him everywhere from New Zealand to Australia, China, South Korea, Japan, and all over Europe. For someone who's traveled so much, you'd think he'd love food . . . but the truth? He's one of those people who eats for fuel, and even then, he can sometimes just forget. He loves simple things like avocado toast, a good homemade mac and cheese, and, of course, the Gerard family classic, potato chip chicken. But every single time Red returns home from Europe, he says to me, "Tieghan, you have to make schnitzel. It's my favorite." After hearing this for a couple of years, I finally caved and created this recipe. My trick is using panko bread crumbs for an extra-crispy schnitzel and tossing in some broccoli for a vibrant finish.

4 boneless pork chops, about ½ inch thick

Kosher salt and freshly ground pepper

2½ cups panko bread crumbs

2 teaspoons garlic powder

1 teaspoon paprika

4 tablespoons extra-virgin olive oil

3 tablespoons salted butter

1 lemon, sliced

1 head of broccoli, cut into florets

Fresh thyme leaves, for serving

Flaky sea salt, for serving

1. Season the pork with salt and pepper. In a shallow medium bowl, combine the panko, garlic powder, paprika, and a pinch each of salt and pepper. Working with one chop at a time, press the pork into the panko, using your fist to pound the crumbs into the pork. Repeat with the remaining pork chops.

2. Heat the olive oil in a large skillet over medium-high heat. When the oil shimmers, add 2 of the chops and cook until deep golden brown on both sides, 3 to 4 minutes per side. Transfer the schnitzel to a paper towel–lined plate to drain, and repeat the frying process with the remaining 2 pork chops.

3. Wipe the skillet clean and add the butter and lemon slices. Sear the lemon until golden on each side, about 1 minute per side. Remove the lemon from the skillet and add to the plate with the schnitzel.

4. Place the broccoli in the same skillet and season with salt and pepper. Cook until charred on the edges and tender, about 5 minutes. Remove from the heat.

5. Serve each schnitzel with broccoli, lemon slices, fresh thyme leaves, and a sprinkle of flaky salt.

. . . .

Serve with my oven-baked Cajun fries (see page 58).

INSTANT CHICKEN GUMBO

SERVES: 6 TO 8

PREP TIME: 15 minutes
COOK TIME: See specific device method

I was fourteen when I first began making this recipe, and it's been a Top 5 Gerard family favorite ever since. In fact, there's not a meal in the universe my brother Brendan loves more than this gumbo. Every time he's home in Colorado, I *have* to make this for him. The recipe was originally shared with me through my mom's best friend, Mrs. Mooney (you may remember her penne from my first cookbook). The original calls for a lot of stirring and a very long time on the stove. I was hesitant to attempt to simplify it, but I am so glad I did. This gumbo is every bit as delicious as the original and impresses everyone I've served it to—including Brendan! The pressure cooker significantly cuts down the amount of work and time involved yet still creates a flavorful gumbo with perfectly cooked chicken. Serve this over rice with a side of your favorite bread. It's the perfect Cajun meal.

¾ cup canola oil

¾ cup all-purpose flour

3 red, orange, and/or yellow bell peppers, seeded and sliced

2 celery stalks, diced

4 garlic cloves, minced or grated

1 medium yellow onion, diced

1 (14-ounce) can fire-roasted diced tomatoes

1 tablespoon dried oregano

1 tablespoon dried thyme

1 tablespoon dried basil

1 tablespoon Homemade Creole Seasoning (page 58) or store-bought blend

1 teaspoon chili powder

1 to 2 teaspoons ground cayenne pepper

Kosher salt and freshly ground pepper

6 cups low-sodium chicken broth

3 andouille sausage links, halved and sliced

3 skinless, bone-in chicken thighs

3 cups cooked rice, for serving

Fresh parsley, for serving

SLOW COOKER COOK TIME: 5 to 8 hours

1. In a medium skillet, whisk together the oil and flour over medium heat and cook, stirring occasionally, until the roux is combined and golden brown, about 10 minutes. Transfer the roux to the slow cooker pot.

2. Stir in the bell peppers, celery, garlic, onion, tomatoes, oregano, thyme, basil, Creole seasoning, chili powder, cayenne, and a large pinch each of salt and pepper. Add the broth, sausage, and chicken. Cover and cook until the chicken is falling off the bones, 6 to 8 hours on low, or 5 to 6 hours on high. Remove the chicken bones and discard.

3. Cook, uncovered, over high heat until the gumbo has thickened, 20 to 30 minutes.

4. Divide the rice among six to eight bowls and ladle the gumbo over the rice. Garnish with parsley. Store any leftovers refrigerated in an airtight container for up to 3 days.

PRESSURE COOKER COOK TIME: 50 minutes, plus additional time to come to pressure

1. Using the sauté function, whisk together the oil and flour in the pressure cooker pot and cook, stirring occasionally, until the roux is combined and golden brown, about 10 minutes.

2. Stir in the bell peppers, celery, garlic, onion, tomatoes, oregano, thyme, basil, Creole seasoning, chili powder, cayenne, and a large pinch each of salt and pepper. Add the broth, sausage, and chicken. Lock the lid in place and cook on high pressure for 35 minutes. Quick or natural release, then open when the pressure subsides. Remove the chicken bones and discard.

3. Using the sauté function, bring the gumbo to a boil and cook until thickened, about 5 minutes.

4. Finish as directed for the slow cooker.

STOVETOP COOK TIME: 3 hours 30 minutes

1. In a large pot, whisk together the oil and flour over medium heat and cook until the mixture turns golden brown, 15 to 20 minutes.

2. Stir in the bell peppers, celery, garlic, onion, tomatoes, oregano, thyme, basil, Creole seasoning, chili powder, cayenne, and a large pinch each of salt and pepper. The roux will bubble and thicken up immediately into a paste that coats the vegetables. Let the veggies cook over medium heat, stirring occasionally, until they begin to soften, about 5 minutes. Add the broth, sausage, and chicken. Bring the gumbo to a boil, reduce the heat, and simmer, covered, until the chicken is falling apart, at least 3 hours or up to all day (the longer the better for flavors to blend). Skim the fat off the top and remove and discard the bones.

3. Finish as directed for the slow cooker.

BROWNED SAGE-BUTTER CHICKEN POT PIE

SERVES: 6

PREP TIME: 20 minutes
COOK TIME: 1 hour 10 minutes
TOTAL TIME: 1 hour 30 minutes

This might come as a shock, but the idea of chicken pot pie has never excited me. Honestly, every pot pie recipe I've ever looked at has always seemed a little . . . bland. I've never understood why everyone gets so excited about chicken and peas baked under a crust. Where is the flavor, you know? Well, I finally decided to try my hand at a pot pie, but I made some tweaks that made all the difference. This isn't your grandma's pot pie—it's so much better. Hello, browned sage butter, broccoli, and buttery, flaky puff pastry. Yes, please.

4 tablespoons salted butter

1 shallot, chopped

2 tablespoons chopped fresh sage, plus whole leaves for serving

1 tablespoon fresh thyme leaves

⅓ cup all-purpose flour

3 cups low-sodium chicken broth

1 cup whole milk

Kosher salt and freshly ground pepper

6 carrots, chopped

1 cup broccoli florets, roughly chopped

1 to 2 cups shredded rotisserie chicken, store-bought or homemade (see page 178)

¼ cup fresh parsley, roughly chopped

1 sheet frozen puff pastry, thawed (see Note)

1 large egg, beaten

1. Preheat the oven to 375°F.

2. In a large oven-safe skillet, melt the butter over medium heat. Add the shallot, chopped sage, and thyme and cook, stirring often, until the shallot is fragrant and the butter is lightly browned, 3 to 5 minutes. Add the flour and cook until golden, 1 to 2 minutes. Gradually whisk in the broth and milk, season with salt and pepper, and bring to a boil.

3. Reduce the heat to medium-low and simmer, whisking occasionally, until the sauce thickens slightly, about 10 minutes. Stir in the carrots and broccoli and cook until just tender, about 5 minutes more.

4. Remove the skillet from the heat and add the chicken and parsley. Taste and add more salt and pepper as needed.

5. Unfold the puff pastry and gently roll it out on a lightly floured work surface until it is slightly larger than your skillet. Place the pastry over the skillet, tucking the sides under the top to fit, and brush with egg. Make 2 or 3 slits in the top of the pastry with a sharp knife.

6. Bake until the pastry is golden brown, 40 to 45 minutes. Let cool 10 minutes and sprinkle with sage leaves before serving.

7. Store any leftovers refrigerated covered in plastic wrap or aluminum foil for up to 3 days.

. . . .

When working with puff pastry, cover any pastry that is not being used with a damp towel to keep it from drying out while you work. The pastry should never sit uncovered.

BREADED LEMON CHICKEN

WITH BURST CHERRY TOMATOES

SERVES: 4

PREP TIME: 10 minutes
COOK TIME: 30 minutes
TOTAL TIME: 40 minutes

The easiest way to make chicken breasts less boring? Bread them, add lots of lemon and pepper, and use cherry tomatoes to make a mouthwatering pan sauce. Oh, and add some butter and garlic, too (when in doubt, butter is always a good idea). This one-skillet dinner comes together in minutes. It's best for the summertime months, when cherry tomatoes and fresh basil are overflowing at the local markets, but to be honest, I often make this in the dead of winter, too, just to remind myself that warmer days are to come. If you want to go above and beyond, finish this off with some cheese. I'm rather fond of a dusting of Parmesan, or maybe even some crumbled feta.

1½ pounds boneless, skinless chicken breasts

3 tablespoons extra-virgin olive oil

Zest and juice of 1 lemon

Kosher salt and freshly ground pepper

½ cup all-purpose flour

3 tablespoons salted butter

½ lemon, sliced

3 cups cherry tomatoes

4 garlic cloves, smashed

2 tablespoons fresh thyme leaves

Crushed red pepper flakes

½ cup dry white wine, such as pinot grigio or Sauvignon Blanc (see Note)

1 large handful of fresh basil leaves, roughly chopped

1. Rub the chicken all over with 1 tablespoon of the olive oil and the lemon zest, and season generously with salt and pepper. Sprinkle the flour evenly over the chicken, pressing it to adhere.

2. Heat the remaining 2 tablespoons of olive oil in a large skillet over medium-high heat. When the oil shimmers, add the chicken and sear until golden, about 5 minutes per side. Remove the chicken from the skillet and set it aside on a large plate.

3. In the same skillet, combine the butter and lemon slices. Sear the lemon until caramelized, about 30 seconds per side. Remove the lemon from the pan and set it aside with the chicken.

4. Increase the heat under the skillet to high and add the tomatoes, garlic, thyme, and a pinch each of salt, pepper, and red pepper flakes. Cook until the tomatoes begin to burst, 4 to 5 minutes. Reduce the heat to medium-low and stir in the wine and lemon juice, scraping up any browned bits from the bottom. Return the chicken to the skillet, increase the heat to medium, and simmer until the chicken is cooked through, 10 to 15 minutes.

5. Transfer the chicken to a serving platter and top it with basil and the caramelized lemon slices. Spoon the sauce over the top and scatter the tomatoes all around.

. . . .

If you'd like to swap out the wine in this recipe, I recommend using ¼ cup of apple cider or champagne vinegar and ¼ cup of low-sodium chicken broth. You can also use all chicken broth if you prefer, but I love the acidity from the vinegar.

GINGERED APPLE PORK CHOPS

SERVES: 4

PREP TIME: 10 minutes
COOK TIME: 30 minutes
TOTAL TIME: 40 minutes,
plus resting time

Here's the deal—I love a good skillet chicken. But as much as I love a good skillet chicken, I also love a good skillet pork chop. Sometimes chicken just doesn't cut it, and you need something different but still impressive. This is that recipe. It's best suited for the fall months when apples are in season. It's tangy and spicy and boasts a pan sauce that's a true delight, so be sure to spoon it over every inch of these chops.

2 tablespoons extra-virgin olive oil

2 bone-in pork chops, about 1 inch thick and 8 to 10 ounces each

Kosher salt and freshly ground pepper

1 medium yellow onion, diced

2 garlic cloves, smashed

1 inch fresh ginger, grated or chopped

2 teaspoons cumin seeds

½ cup apple cider

2 tablespoons apple cider vinegar

1 to 2 jalapeño or red Fresno peppers, seeded and sliced

4 sprigs of fresh thyme

1 Honeycrisp apple, cored and cut into ¼-inch slices

1 cup red grapes

3 tablespoons salted butter

1. Preheat the oven to 450°F.

2. In a large cast-iron skillet, heat the olive oil on medium-high heat. Season the pork chops with salt and pepper. When the oil shimmers, add the chops and sear until browned on both sides, 3 to 5 minutes per side. Transfer the chops to a plate.

3. In the same skillet, combine the onion, garlic, ginger, and cumin seeds and cook, stirring occasionally, until the onion is fragrant and the cumin seeds are toasted, about 5 minutes. Pour in the cider and vinegar, scraping up any browned bits from the bottom of the pan. Increase the heat to high, bring the cider mixture to a boil, then reduce the heat to low.

4. Slide the pork chops and any collected juices back into the skillet. Add the jalapeños and thyme and sprinkle the apples and grapes around the pork. Transfer the skillet to the oven and roast until an instant-read thermometer inserted horizontally into the center of the meat registers 135°F, 10 to 15 minutes.

5. Remove the skillet from the oven. Add the butter and let it melt over the pork chops.

6. Let the chops sit 5 minutes, then cut away the bone in each and cut them into ¼-inch-thick slices. To serve, divide the pork, apples, and grapes among four plates and spoon the pan sauce over the tops.

PAPRIKA-RUBBED "ROTISSERIE" CHICKEN

SERVES: 4

PREP TIME: 15 minutes
COOK TIME: See specific device method

Rotisserie chicken wasn't something I ever thought I needed in my life, but my Nonnie taught me otherwise. She'd often buy a whole rotisserie chicken from the grocery store to enjoy for lunch and then use the leftovers for dinner that night, mixing the shredded chicken into soups, homemade enchiladas, or even nachos. Genius, right? I wondered if I could duplicate that standard rotisserie chicken at home to make on Sundays for meal prep. After a little trial and error, I discovered that my pressure cooker made the most deliciously moist "rotisserie" chicken. I now make this dish on weekends, or sometimes as an easy dinner alongside a serving of Oven-Baked Cajun Fries (page 58). I'll then use the leftover meat throughout the week in my Browned Sage-Butter Chicken Pot Pie (page 173) or my Sun-Dried Tomato and Avocado Salad with Chicken (page 79). The ways to use this chicken are endless: it's your new back-pocket chicken dish.

Zest of 1 lemon

1 tablespoon fresh thyme leaves

1 tablespoon smoked paprika

2 teaspoons chili powder

1 teaspoon garlic powder

1 teaspoon onion powder

1 to 2 teaspoons ground cayenne pepper

Kosher salt and freshly ground pepper

1 whole chicken (4 to 5 pounds; see Note)

1 tablespoon extra-virgin olive oil

1 cup dry white wine, such as pinot grigio or Sauvignon Blanc, or low-sodium chicken broth

1 lemon, halved

SLOW COOKER COOK TIME: 4 to 8 hours

1. In a small bowl, stir together the lemon zest, thyme, paprika, chili powder, garlic powder, onion powder, cayenne, and a pinch each of salt and pepper.

2. Remove the giblets from the chicken and discard. Pat the chicken dry and rub all over with the olive oil. Rub the spice mixture all over the chicken.

3. Place the chicken in the slow cooker pot breast side up. Pour the wine all around the chicken. Add the lemon. Cover and cook until the chicken is cooked through and reaches an internal temperature of 160°F, 6 to 8 hours on low, or 4 to 5 hours on high.

4. Transfer the chicken to a plate and let it rest for about 5 minutes. Serve warm immediately, or shred and store refrigerated in an airtight container with any juices left in the slow cooker bowl for up to 3 days.

PRESSURE COOKER COOK TIME: 35 minutes, plus additional time to come to pressure

1. In a small bowl, stir together the lemon zest, thyme, paprika, chili powder, garlic powder, onion powder, cayenne, and a pinch each of salt and pepper.

2. Remove the giblets from the chicken and discard. Pat the chicken dry and rub all over with the olive oil. Rub the spice mixture all over the chicken.

3. Using the sauté function, place the chicken in the pressure cooker pot, breast side down. Sear the chicken on one side until browned, 3 to 5 minutes, then flip and cook until browned on the other side, 3 to 4 minutes more. Pour the wine all around the chicken and add the lemon. Lock the lid in place and cook on high pressure for 25 minutes. Quick or natural release, then open when the pressure subsides.

4. Finish as directed for the slow cooker.

. . . .

If you're using a chicken larger than 4 to 5 pounds, tack on 5 minutes of cooking time per pound.

OVEN ROASTING COOK TIME: 3 hours

1. Preheat the oven to 300°F.

2. In a small bowl, stir together the lemon zest, thyme, paprika, chili powder, garlic powder, onion powder, cayenne, and a pinch each of salt and pepper.

3. Remove the giblets from the chicken and discard. Place the chicken in a large oven-safe skillet or roasting pan. Pat the chicken dry and rub all over with the olive oil. Rub the spice mixture all over the chicken. Pour the wine all around the chicken and add the lemon.

4. Transfer to the oven and roast, spooning any juices in the pan over the bird halfway through cooking, until the chicken is cooked through and reaches an internal temperature of 160°F, 2 hours 45 minutes to 3 hours, depending on the size of your bird.

5. Let the chicken rest for 10 minutes before carving and serving.

6. Serve warm immediately, or shred and store refrigerated in an airtight container with any juices left in the roasting pan for up to 3 days.

ROSEMARY-PEACH BRUSCHETTA CHICKEN

SERVES: 6

PREP TIME: 15 minutes
COOK TIME: 30 minutes
TOTAL TIME: 45 minutes

Sure, peaches are great in pies, but they can be used for so much more than baking. In fact, my personal favorite is the sweet *and* savory route. Are you surprised? Yep, I love a sweet-and-savory dinner, which is why I created this recipe. Pan-seared chicken and crispy bacon make for the most delicious combination alongside juicy summer peaches. Sprinkle on some mozzarella and spoon on fresh basil and tomatoes. And that's how to *really* do up those summertime peaches!

1½ pounds boneless, skinless chicken breasts

1 tablespoon extra-virgin olive oil

1 tablespoon chopped fresh rosemary

Zest and juice of 1 lemon

Kosher salt and freshly ground pepper

4 slices thick-cut bacon, quartered

1 shallot, thinly sliced

1 cup dry white wine or low-sodium chicken broth

2 peaches, sliced

1 cup fresh cherry-size mozzarella balls

2 cups cherry tomatoes, halved

1 cup fresh basil leaves, roughly chopped

2 tablespoons balsamic vinegar

1. Preheat the oven to 425°F.

2. Rub the chicken all over with the olive oil, rosemary, and lemon zest and season generously with salt and pepper.

3. Place the bacon in a large, oven-safe skillet over medium heat. Cook until the fat renders and the bacon is crispy, about 5 minutes. Remove the bacon from the skillet and drain on a paper towel–lined plate.

4. Add the chicken to the fat in the skillet and sear until golden, about 5 minutes per side. Stir in the shallot and cook until fragrant, about 2 minutes. Reduce the heat to medium-low and add the wine and lemon juice, scraping up any browned bits from the bottom of the pan. Simmer until the sauce has been reduced by about one-third, about 10 minutes. Return the bacon to the skillet and arrange the peaches and mozzarella evenly around the chicken. Transfer the skillet to the oven and roast until the peaches are just charred on the edges and the cheese has melted, about 5 minutes.

5. Top with the tomatoes, basil, and vinegar. Spoon the pan sauces over the chicken and serve warm, family-style.

CHICKEN TINGA TACOS

SERVES: 6

PREP TIME: 5 minutes
COOK TIME: 20 minutes
TOTAL TIME: 25 minutes

Growing up, my brothers and I would eat tacos for dinner at least once a week. Of course, we all still love a good taco today—who doesn't? Over the years I've learned how to make a much better taco, and these chicken tinga tacos are a true essential in my dinner lineup. I've made them using a few staples I always have lying around: onions, enchilada sauce, and chipotle peppers in adobo. What really makes a tinga taco is that smoky chipotle flavor, so don't be shy with the chipotle peppers. Their flavor is more smoky than spicy, so even if you're sensitive to spice, you can still use them, but start off with one pepper and work your way up to two if you feel you can handle the heat. Serve these topped with sweet-and-spicy pineapple salsa, mashed avocado, and a little crumbled feta.

2 tablespoons extra-virgin olive oil

1½ pounds boneless, skinless chicken breast

1 medium onion, finely chopped

Kosher salt and freshly ground pepper

1½ cups red enchilada sauce

2 to 4 chipotle peppers in adobo

1 avocado, mashed

8 to 12 tortillas, warmed

Pickled Jalapeño Pineapple Salsa (page 49) or store-bought salsa, for serving (optional)

4 ounces crumbled feta, for serving

Cilantro, for serving

1. Heat the olive oil in a medium saucepan over medium heat. When the oil shimmers, add the chicken, onion, and a pinch each of salt and pepper. Cook, stirring the onion and turning the chicken occasionally, until the chicken is browned all over and the onion is fragrant, 3 to 5 minutes per side. Stir in the enchilada sauce and the chipotle peppers. Cover, reduce the heat to low, and simmer until the chicken is cooked through and tender, about 15 minutes. Remove the pan from the heat and, using two forks, shred the chicken directly in the pan.

2. To serve, spread the mashed avocado over the tortillas, dividing evenly, and add the chicken on top. Top with salsa (if desired), cheese, and cilantro.

COCONUT CHICKEN TIKKA MASALA

SERVES: 6

PREP TIME: 15 minutes
COOK TIME: 30 minutes
TOTAL TIME: 45 minutes

If you often find yourself heading to your favorite local Indian spot for curry and fresh naan, you definitely need to try this recipe. It is healthier, has incredible flavor, and can be made using a handful of pantry staple ingredients you probably have on hand right now. My secret is to blend up a quick homemade yellow curry paste, which becomes the base flavor. Coconut milk keeps the masala creamy and adds a hint of coconut flavor, which I always find nice with Indian cuisine. The great thing is that the flavors get even better the next day, meaning leftovers are especially delicious.

CURRY PASTE

1 medium yellow onion, quartered

1 shallot, halved

6 garlic cloves

2 (1-inch) pieces of fresh ginger, peeled

3 tablespoons garam masala

2 teaspoons ground turmeric

2 teaspoons kosher salt

1 teaspoon crushed red pepper flakes

Zest of 1 lemon

CHICKEN

2 pounds boneless, skinless chicken breast, cubed

½ cup full-fat plain Greek yogurt

1 (14-ounce) can full-fat unsweetened coconut milk

1 (6-ounce) can tomato paste

¼ cup cilantro, chopped

3 cups cooked rice, for serving

1. **Make the curry paste.** In a blender or food processor, combine the onion, shallot, garlic, ginger, garam masala, turmeric, salt, red pepper flakes, and lemon zest and pulse until a smooth paste forms, about 1 minute.

2. **Make the chicken.** In a gallon-size zip-top bag, combine 2 tablespoons of the curry paste, the chicken, and the yogurt. Seal the bag and massage the mixture into the chicken to cover completely. Marinate at room temperature for 30 minutes or refrigerate up to overnight.

3. Heat a large, high-sided skillet over medium heat. Add ¼ cup of the curry paste and cook until fragrant, about 1 minute. Stir in the marinated chicken, coconut milk, and tomato paste. Cover and cook until the chicken is cooked through, 15 to 20 minutes. Remove the lid and simmer until the sauce thickens slightly, about 5 minutes more.

4. Stir in the cilantro and serve the chicken over rice.

. . . .

You can double the curry paste and store it refrigerated in an airtight container for up to 1 month, or in the freezer for up to 4 months. Thaw in the fridge overnight.

SAGE CHICKEN

WITH CREAMY POTATOES

SERVES: 4

PREP TIME: 10 minutes
COOK TIME: 45 minutes
TOTAL TIME: 55 minutes

As soon as I made this recipe I knew I had to share it with you. Let me put it into perspective: the recipe starts off by crisping up bacon and ends with potatoes, a splash of wine, and cheese. Who could not love that? It's the easiest and maybe best-ever one-pan dinner. Anyone who enjoys roasted chicken and potatoes will absolutely love this dish. And did I mention it's ready in just about an hour? My idea of dinnertime perfection.

2 pounds skin-on, bone-in chicken breasts

Kosher salt and freshly ground pepper

3 slices thick-cut bacon, chopped

2 tablespoons extra-virgin olive oil

3 garlic cloves, smashed

2 tablespoons chopped fresh sage leaves

1 pound mixed baby potatoes, halved if large

2 cups dry white wine, such as pinot grigio or Sauvignon Blanc

1 cup heavy cream

2 tablespoons Dijon mustard

½ cup grated Parmesan cheese, plus more for serving

1 tablespoon fresh thyme leaves, plus 2 sprigs, for serving

1. Preheat the oven to 400°F.

2. Season the chicken with salt and pepper.

3. Place the bacon in a large Dutch oven or cast-iron skillet and cook over medium heat until the fat renders and the bacon is crispy, about 5 minutes. Remove the bacon from the skillet and drain on a paper towel–lined plate. Wipe the skillet clean.

4. In the same pan, heat the olive oil over high heat. When the oil shimmers, add the chicken and sear until golden, 3 to 5 minutes per side. Stir in the garlic and sage and cook until fragrant, about 1 minute more.

5. Scatter the potatoes around the chicken and add the wine, cream, mustard, and Parmesan. Season with salt and pepper. Bring to a boil and reduce the heat to low. Sprinkle in the thyme leaves and crispy bacon.

6. Transfer the pan to the oven and roast until the chicken is cooked through and the potatoes are fork-tender, 25 to 30 minutes. Remove the garlic cloves and discard.

7. Garnish with the thyme sprigs and Parmesan and serve.

. . . .

The cream sauce leans more toward a wine flavor than a cream flavor, which I find particularly nice. If you'd like to use less wine, or no wine at all, low-sodium chicken broth can take its place.

CAROLINE'S FAMILY'S CHICKEN MOSTACCIOLI

SERVES: 6 TO 8

PREP TIME: 15 minutes
COOK TIME: 2 hours 30 minutes
TOTAL TIME: 2 hours 45 minutes

I feel pretty lucky to have such a tight-knit family that has grown over the years to include a sister-in-law, girlfriends, and boyfriends. This recipe comes from my cousin Matt's longtime girlfriend, Caroline. Coincidentally, Caroline's parents grew up with mine—they've all known each other since they were kids. I guess that's small-town living for you! One Christmas, Caroline taught me how to make her family's chicken mostaccioli ("little mustaches" in Italian). With just a glance at the ingredient list, you might not think it's anything out of the ordinary, but let me tell you, this chicken is legitimately the best ever. Her family's secret is to slowly cook the chicken for hours, until it's falling off the bone and shreds with little effort. The bacon, allspice, and bay leaves keep the sauce rich. If time allows, make this in the morning, or even the day before you plan to serve it. The longer it sits, the more flavor it will have.

20 whole allspice berries

4 slices thick-cut bacon, chopped

1 large yellow onion, chopped

4 garlic cloves, smashed

2 bone-in, skin-on chicken breasts (about 1½ pounds)

2 or 3 bone-in skin-on chicken thighs (about 1 pound)

Kosher salt and freshly ground pepper

1 cup dry red wine, such as Pinot Noir

2 (6-ounce) cans tomato paste

2 bay leaves

1 Parmesan rind, plus grated Parmesan for serving

1 pound mostaccioli pasta

1. Wrap the allspice in a piece of cheesecloth and secure with kitchen twine.

2. In a large Dutch oven or saucepan, cook the bacon on medium-high heat until the fat has rendered and the bacon is beginning to crisp, 5 to 8 minutes. Stir in the onion and garlic. Add the chicken breasts and thighs. Season with salt and pepper. Cook until the chicken is browned, about 5 minutes per side. Pour in the wine, scraping up any browned bits from the bottom of the pan.

3. Add the tomato paste and 4 cups of water, stirring until combined. Add the bay leaves, Parmesan rind, and allspice. Cover the pan and reduce the heat to low. Simmer for 2 hours without any peeking. After 2 hours, lift the lid and stir the sauce. At this point, the chicken should be falling apart. You can continue to simmer the sauce over low heat 2 to 4 hours more, if you have time, or proceed as directed in step 4.

4. Remove the bay leaves, Parmesan rind, allspice, and chicken from the sauce. Discard the bay leaves, rind, and allspice. Using two forks, shred the chicken, discarding the skin and bones, and return it to the sauce. Taste and add more salt and pepper as needed.

5. Meanwhile, bring a large pot of salted water to a boil. Cook the pasta according to the package directions, until al dente. Drain.

6. Serve the chicken over the pasta topped with grated Parmesan.

7. Store any leftovers refrigerated in an airtight container for up to 3 days.

While the recipe calls for mostaccioli pasta, I've found good ole ziti or penne works just as well.

WHITE WINE-BRAISED
CHICKEN
WITH ARTICHOKES AND ORZO

. . . .
SERVES: 6
. . . .

PREP TIME: 15 minutes
COOK TIME: 30 minutes
TOTAL TIME: 45 minutes

When your family loves a dinner of chicken and rice as much as mine does, you have to find new ways to serve it so no one gets bored. This is a dinner of chicken and rice, but it's way better than anything you'd expect. It's Greek inspired, made with orzo pasta, finished with feta cheese, and all in one skillet. I first made this on a rainy spring day when all I had in my pantry was a jar of marinated artichokes and salty green olives. It was one of those dishes where I threw a bunch of stuff together, hoped it would turn out edible, and ended up with something delicious. It's now a family favorite.

2 tablespoons extra-virgin olive oil

1½ pounds boneless, skinless chicken breasts or thighs

Kosher salt and freshly ground pepper

2 tablespoons salted butter

4 garlic cloves, minced or grated

1 cup dry orzo

1 cup dry white wine, such as pinot grigio or Sauvignon Blanc

1¼ cups low-sodium chicken broth

1 (8-ounce) jar marinated artichoke hearts, drained and roughly chopped

½ cup pitted green olives

Zest and juice of 1 lemon

½ cup cubed or crumbled feta cheese, for serving

1 tablespoon chopped fresh dill, for serving

1. Preheat the oven to 400°F.

2. Heat the olive oil in a large Dutch oven or cast-iron skillet over medium-high heat. Season the chicken all over with salt and pepper. When the oil shimmers, add the chicken and sear until golden, 3 to 5 minutes per side. Transfer the chicken to a large plate.

3. In the same pan, combine the butter, garlic, and orzo and cook until the garlic is fragrant and the orzo is toasted, 2 to 3 minutes. Add the wine to the skillet and scrape up any browned bits from the bottom of the pan. Stir in the chicken broth, artichokes, green olives, lemon zest, and lemon juice. Increase the heat to high and bring to a boil.

4. Return the chicken and any collected juices to the pan. Transfer to the oven and roast until the chicken is completely cooked through, about 15 minutes.

5. Divide the chicken and sauce among six plates, top with feta and fresh dill, and serve.

KAI'S FAVORITE SESAME-ORANGE CHICKEN

SERVES: 4

PREP TIME: 15 minutes
COOK TIME: 15 minutes
TOTAL TIME: 30 minutes

I've always been a people pleaser—and since I was thirteen years old, food has been my way of making those around me happy. I always take requests. Case in point: this orange chicken. Where we live in the Colorado mountains, we definitely do not have a Panda Express. So when my brother Kai requested I make one of his favorite greasy airport meals, orange chicken, I naturally obliged. Of course, I put my own twists on the dish, adding in lots of sesame, fresh ginger, and an extra shot of citrus. I opted to pan-fry the chicken versus deep-fry. The verdict? It could not have turned out better—Kai actually deemed it better than the original.

1½ pounds boneless, skinless chicken breast, cut into bite-size pieces

4 tablespoons low-sodium soy sauce

¼ cup all-purpose flour

1 (1-inch) piece of fresh ginger, peeled and grated

2 garlic cloves, grated

Zest and juice of ½ orange

2 tablespoons hoisin sauce

2 tablespoons rice vinegar

1 to 2 teaspoons crushed red pepper flakes

1 tablespoon toasted sesame oil

2 tablespoons extra-virgin olive oil

2 green onions, chopped, plus more for serving

Steamed white or brown rice, for serving

2 tablespoons toasted sesame seeds, for serving

1. In a medium bowl, combine the chicken, 2 tablespoons of the soy sauce, and the flour. Toss, making sure the flour has evenly coated the chicken.

2. In a small bowl or glass measuring cup, whisk together the remaining 2 tablespoons of soy sauce and the ginger, garlic, orange zest, orange juice, hoisin sauce, vinegar, red pepper flakes, and toasted sesame oil.

3. Heat the olive oil in a large skillet over medium-high heat. When the oil shimmers, add the chicken in an even layer and cook, stirring, until browned all over, about 5 minutes. Pour in the sauce and bring to a boil, then reduce the heat to medium-low and simmer, stirring occasionally, until the sauce thickens and the chicken is coated, 5 to 10 minutes. Remove the skillet from the heat and stir in the green onions.

4. Serve the chicken over rice and top with more green onions and toasted sesame seeds.

You could also make this dish with frozen shrimp or even a head of cauliflower broken into florets for a vegetarian option. All are equally delicious.

QUICK FILIPINO ADOBO

SERVES: 6

PREP TIME: 10 minutes
COOK TIME: 50 minutes
TOTAL TIME: 1 hour

I can't take credit for this recipe. Well, sure, I added a few touches, but mostly it comes from Hailey, my brother Red's girlfriend. When I first met Hailey, we immediately bonded over our love of food. Unlike my brother, she has an adventurous palate, so she's awesome when it comes to talking recipes. Hailey's mom is from the Philippines, and as I got to know her more, I was introduced to Filipino cooking. Until Hailey, I wasn't too familiar with traditional Filipino dishes and while I still have a lot to explore, I can tell you that a traditional pork adobo is a good place to start. Not only is adobo one of the simplest meals, it is mouthwateringly good, too. Traditionally, adobo is pork marinated and braised in a mixture of soy sauce and vinegar. It's a little bit sweet, a touch tangy, and completely full of flavor. I kept this recipe as traditional as I could, only swapping out the brown sugar for honey, adding pineapple chunks, and serving each plate with fresh jalapeños for some heat.

2 pounds pork shoulder or butt, cut into 1½- to 2-inch cubes

Freshly ground pepper

¾ cup low-sodium soy sauce

⅓ cup white vinegar

¼ cup honey

2 tablespoons extra-virgin olive oil

6 garlic cloves, minced or grated

4 dried bay leaves

1 cup fresh pineapple chunks

Coconut Rice (recipe follows), for serving

1 to 2 jalapeño peppers, seeded and sliced, for serving (optional)

1. Season the pork all over with pepper. In a large glass measuring cup, combine the soy sauce, vinegar, honey, and 1 cup of water.

2. Heat the olive oil in a large, high-sided skillet over high heat. When the oil shimmers, add the pork, working in batches, and sear on all sides, about 2 minutes per side.

3. Return all the pork back to the skillet and add the garlic. Cook until fragrant, 1 to 2 minutes. Reduce the heat to low and pour in the soy sauce mixture. Add the bay leaves. Cover and simmer over low heat until the pork is cooked through and the sauce is thickening, 30 to 40 minutes. If the sauce is thickening too fast, add up to ¼ cup of water. Remove the lid and stir in the pineapple, tossing to coat. Remove from the heat.

4. Remove and discard the bay leaves. Serve the adobo over coconut rice and top with jalapeños, if desired.

<10

COCONUT RICE

1 (14-ounce) can full-fat unsweetened coconut milk

1 cup uncooked jasmine rice

1. Combine the coconut milk and ½ cup of water in a medium pot and bring to a boil over high heat. Add the rice. Stir to combine, place the lid on the pot, and turn the heat down to the lowest setting possible. Allow the rice to cook 10 minutes on low, then turn the heat off completely. Let the rice sit, covered, 15 minutes more. (Don't peek inside!)

2. Remove the lid and fluff the rice with a fork.

While pork is traditional in adobo, it is often made with chicken as well. You can use whole chicken thighs or breasts in place of cubed pork if you prefer.

SUN-DRIED TOMATO TURKEY MEATBALL BAKE

SERVES: 8

PREP TIME: 25 minutes
COOK TIME: 1 hour
TOTAL TIME: 1 hour 25 minutes

I'm going to come right out and say it: *Meatball* has to be one of my least favorite words. It's an odd one, right? You'd think the universe could have thought up something a little more appealing to describe ground meat rolled into a ball, but I guess it is what it is: a ball of meat. Regardless of how I feel about the name, meatballs are loved by many, including me. This one-pan pasta bake makes the classic meatball even better with the addition of cheesy pasta and a one-pan-and-done cooking method. I bake the meatballs and pasta together, omitting the need to pan-fry, meaning no messy stove to clean. You are so welcome.

¾ pound ground turkey

¾ cup whole-milk ricotta cheese

¼ cup grated Parmesan cheese, plus more for serving

¼ cup chopped sun-dried tomatoes packed in olive oil, drained and oil reserved

3 garlic cloves, minced or grated

2 teaspoons dried oregano

Kosher salt and freshly ground pepper

1 (24-ounce) jar marinara sauce

¼ cup balsamic vinegar

3 large eggs, beaten

¾ pound short-cut pasta of your choice

Crushed red pepper flakes

8 ounces low-moisture mozzarella, torn

¼ cup fresh basil leaves, slivered

1. Preheat the oven to 375°F.

2. **Make the meatballs.** In a medium bowl, combine the turkey, ricotta, Parmesan, sun-dried tomatoes, 1 garlic clove, 1 teaspoon of the oregano, and a pinch each of salt and pepper. Using your hands, mix well to combine. Grease your hands with a bit of olive oil and roll the meat into sixteen 2-tablespoon-size balls, placing them in a 9 × 13-inch baking dish.

3. Drizzle the reserved sun-dried tomato oil over the meatballs and place the baking dish in the oven. Bake until the meatballs are crisp on the outside but not yet cooked through, about 10 minutes. Remove the dish from the oven, but leave the oven on.

4. **Make the sauce.** Meanwhile, in a large bowl, combine the marinara sauce, 2 cups of water, the vinegar, eggs, the remaining 2 garlic cloves, the remaining 1 teaspoon of oregano, the pasta, and a pinch of red pepper flakes.

5. Pour the pasta and tomato sauce mixture around the meatballs, gently stirring to distribute. Sprinkle the mozzarella over the top. Cover the baking dish with aluminum foil and bake until the sauce has thickened and the noodles have cooked, about 40 minutes more. Turn the oven to broil, remove the foil, and cook until the top of the bake is golden brown, about 5 minutes.

6. Let the bake cool for 5 minutes, then top with fresh basil and serve.

. . . .

You can also use ground chicken, lean ground pork, or beef in place of the turkey.

BEEF & LAMB

CARNE ASADA TOSTADAS

WITH PICKLED JALAPEÑO PINEAPPLE SALSA

SERVES: 6 TO 8

PREP TIME: 10 minutes
COOK TIME: See specific device method

Before you yell at me, I *know* this dish is not an authentic carne asada, but the taste is spot-on and the recipe is about as easy as it gets. This cookbook *is* titled *Half Baked Harvest Super Simple,* so just go with me. Tossing a flank steak in the slow cooker with onions, garlic, fresh citrus, and spices and then cooking it low and slow yields a beef that shreds easily and tastes delicious. You can use the meat for everything from tacos to burritos to rice bowls, but I love making tostadas for a fun twist on the usual taco night. And the pickled jalapeño pineapple salsa? It's a game changer. I highly recommend enjoying these tostadas with my Spicy Strawberry Paloma (page 73) for a true Mexican-inspired fiesta-style dinner that's doable any night of the week.

2 tablespoons extra-virgin olive oil

2 pounds flank steak

4 garlic cloves, minced or grated

1 large yellow onion, finely chopped

2 teaspoons smoked paprika

2 teaspoons chili powder

Kosher salt and freshly ground pepper

Juice of 1 orange

Juice of 2 limes

½ cup fresh cilantro, chopped

16 tostada or hard taco shells, warmed

FOR SERVING

Mashed avocado

Pickled Jalapeño Pineapple Salsa (page 49) or store-bought salsa

Crumbled cotija cheese

Shredded lettuce

SLOW COOKER COOK TIME: 4 to 6 hours

1. In the slow cooker pot, combine the olive oil, steak, garlic, onion, paprika, chili powder, and a large pinch each of salt and pepper. Massage the seasoning into the steak with your hands until evenly distributed, 3 to 5 minutes. Add the orange and lime juices.

2. Cover and cook until the meat is falling apart, about 6 hours on low, or about 4 hours on high. Remove the steak from the slow cooker and let it rest on a cutting board for 15 minutes. Using two forks, shred the meat, return it to the slow cooker, add the cilantro, and toss to combine.

3. To serve, spread each tostada shell with avocado and top with the meat, salsa, cheese, and lettuce.

4. Store any leftovers refrigerated in an airtight container for up to 3 days.

PRESSURE COOKER COOK TIME: 15 minutes, plus additional time to come to pressure

1. In the pressure cooker pot, combine the olive oil, steak, garlic, onion, paprika, chili powder, and a large pinch each of salt and pepper. Massage the seasoning into the steak with your hands until evenly distributed, 3 to 5 minutes. Add the orange and lime juices.

2. Lock the lid in place and cook on high pressure for 10 minutes. Quick or natural release, then open when the pressure subsides. Remove the steak from the pressure cooker pot and let it rest on a cutting board for 15 minutes. Using two forks, shred the meat, return it to the pot, add the cilantro, and toss to combine.

3. Finish as directed for the slow cooker.

POBLANO CHILI

SERVES: 8

PREP TIME: 15 minutes
COOK TIME: See specific device method

I am a firm believer that everyone needs a really good chili in their recipe box. This is my really good chili. I make it whenever I have a hungry group of snowboarders to feed (which is rather often during the long snowy season) and for Sunday night dinners throughout the fall and winter. Poblano peppers give the chili a touch of smoky flavor, and I like to keep it well spiced with both chipotle chile powder and regular chili powder. If you can, make this the day before you plan to serve it—chili is always better the more time it has to slowly cook. You can serve this the classic way, in a bowl topped with cheese, or you can serve it the way my mom taught me to eat chili: over angel hair pasta with plenty of cheese melted over the top. P.S. Leftovers make for a delicious batch of nachos the following day.

1 tablespoon extra-virgin olive oil

2 small yellow onions, chopped

4 garlic cloves, minced or grated

2 pounds lean ground beef

2 poblano peppers, seeded and chopped

2 teaspoons chipotle chile powder

2 tablespoons chili powder

1 tablespoon smoked paprika

2 teaspoons ground cumin

½ teaspoon ground cinnamon

1½ teaspoons kosher salt

2 to 3 cups low-sodium chicken broth

1 (28-ounce) can crushed tomatoes, such as San Marzano or Pomi tomatoes

1 (6-ounce) can tomato paste

2 bay leaves

FOR SERVING

Shredded cheddar cheese

Sliced avocado

Sliced green onions

Cilantro

SLOW COOKER COOK TIME: 3 to 7 hours

1. In a large skillet, heat the olive oil over medium heat. When the oil shimmers, add the onions and cook until softened, about 5 minutes. Stir in the garlic and cook until fragrant, about 1 minute more. Add the beef and cook, breaking it up with a wooden spoon, until browned, about 5 minutes.

2. Transfer the beef mixture to the slow cooker pot. Add the poblano peppers, chipotle chile powder, chili powder, smoked paprika, cumin, cinnamon, salt, chicken broth, tomatoes, tomato paste, and bay leaves and stir to combine. Cover and cook until thickened slightly, 5 to 7 hours on low, or 3 to 4 hours on high.

3. Remove and discard the bay leaves and ladle the chili into bowls. Top with cheddar, avocado, green onions, and cilantro.

4. Store any leftovers refrigerated in an airtight container for up to 1 day.

PRESSURE COOKER COOK TIME: 25 minutes, plus additional time to come to pressure

1. Using the sauté function, heat the olive oil and onions in the pressure cooker pot and cook until softened, about 5 minutes. Stir in the garlic and cook until fragrant, about 1 minute more. Add the beef and cook, breaking it up with a wooden spoon, until browned, about 5 minutes.

2. Add the poblano peppers, chipotle chile powder, chili powder, smoked paprika, cumin, cinnamon, salt, chicken broth, tomatoes, tomato paste, and bay leaves and stir to combine. Lock the lid in place and cook on high pressure for 25 minutes. Quick or natural release, then open when the pressure subsides.

3. Finish as directed for the slow cooker.

STOVETOP COOK TIME: 40 minutes to 4 hours

1. Heat the olive oil in a large pot over medium heat. When the oil shimmers, add the onions and cook until softened, about 5 minutes. Stir in the garlic and cook until fragrant, about 1 minute more. Add the beef and cook, breaking it up with a wooden spoon, until browned, about 5 minutes.

2. Add the poblano peppers, chipotle chile powder, chili powder, smoked paprika, cumin, cinnamon, salt, chicken broth, tomatoes, tomato paste, and bay leaves and stir to combine. Cover and cook on low heat, stirring occasionally, until thickened slightly, 30 minutes or up to 4 hours.

3. Finish as directed for the slow cooker.

For whatever reason, most of the people I feed regularly have a serious aversion to beans, so I leave them out of my recipe. If you're like me and love beans, feel free to add a can or two of drained and rinsed black or pinto beans during the last hour or so of cooking.

SPICED LAMB HUMMUS

SERVES: 4 TO 6

PREP TIME: 10 minutes
COOK TIME: 15 minutes
TOTAL TIME: 25 minutes

Have you ever come home from work, opened the fridge, grabbed a container of hummus and a bag of pita chips, and before you realize it, you've eaten the entire thing? It's not just me, right? You've been there, too, I just know it! This dish is my replacement for those "hummus for dinner" nights. It takes a few more minutes to put together, but every extra second is worth it because this hummus is creamy, well spiced, and truly mouthwatering. And while the addition of ground lamb makes it a perfectly acceptable dinner, it's also great served as a party appetizer.

1 pound lean ground lamb

1 medium yellow onion, diced

2 garlic cloves, minced or grated

Zest of 1 lemon

2 teaspoons ground cumin

1 teaspoon smoked paprika

1 teaspoon dried oregano

¼ teaspoon ground cayenne pepper

Kosher salt and freshly ground pepper

⅓ cup fresh parsley, chopped

2 cups Extra-Smooth Hummus (page 69) or store-bought hummus

4 ounces feta or goat cheese, crumbled

Seeds from 1 pomegranate (optional)

Extra-virgin olive oil, for serving

Handful of fresh herbs, for serving

Flatbread or pita chips, for serving

1. In a large skillet, combine the ground lamb and onion and cook over medium-high heat, breaking up the lamb with a wooden spoon, until browned, 5 to 8 minutes. Add the garlic, lemon zest, cumin, paprika, oregano, cayenne, and a pinch each of salt and pepper and sauté until the lamb is cooked through, about 5 minutes more. Remove the skillet from the heat and stir in the parsley. Taste and add more salt and pepper as needed.

2. Divide the hummus among four to six bowls and top with the lamb, feta, pomegranate seeds (if desired), olive oil, and herbs. Serve with flatbread or pita chips for scooping.

SHEET PAN CUBAN STEAK

WITH AVOCADO CHIMICHURRI

SERVES: 6

PREP TIME: 45 minutes
COOK TIME: about 30 minutes
TOTAL TIME: 1 hour 15 minutes,
plus resting time

Sheet pan dinners are a true gift to the world. No matter how many times I think I've made all the sheet pan dinners I can make (enough!), I'll find another combo and then dub it a new "favorite." This Cuban steak, however, is one I make all the time, especially when I'm craving the fresh flavors of warmer climes. That tends to be in April and May, when it's still snowing in Colorado. This steak is marinated in citrus and cooked with potatoes and colorful bell peppers. It's delicious and fun—but what *really* makes this recipe is the chimichurri. I make mine with the addition of avocado and mango, which is definitely not traditional (but that's okay—traditional isn't really my thing). Use any leftover chimichurri for topping grilled meats and seafood, or enjoy it as a dip with tortilla chips.

CUBAN STEAK

2 pounds skirt steak

4 tablespoons extra-virgin olive oil

Juice of 1 lime

Juice of 1 orange

3 garlic cloves

¼ cup chopped fresh oregano

2 bay leaves

1 teaspoon ground cumin

½ teaspoon ground cayenne pepper

Kosher salt and freshly ground pepper

2 russet potatoes, cut into ¼-inch cubes

1 large yellow onion, sliced

1 red or orange bell pepper, sliced

AVOCADO CHIMICHURRI

1 cup fresh cilantro, chopped

1 mango, peeled and diced

1 red Fresno pepper, seeded and chopped

¼ cup red wine vinegar

¼ cup extra-virgin olive oil

Juice of 1 lime

1 avocado, diced

1. **Make the steak.** In a large zip-top bag, combine the steak, 3 tablespoons of the olive oil, the lime juice, orange juice, garlic, oregano, bay leaves, cumin, cayenne, and a pinch each of salt and pepper. Seal the bag and turn to combine. Marinate in the fridge for 30 minutes or up to overnight.

2. Preheat the oven to 450°F with a rack positioned in the upper third of the oven.

3. On a rimmed baking sheet, place the potatoes, onion, bell pepper, the remaining 1 tablespoon of olive oil, and a pinch each of salt and pepper. Gently toss to coat and arrange the vegetables in an even layer, spacing them apart. Roast until the potatoes are golden, about 20 minutes.

4. While the potatoes roast, take the steak out of the fridge and transfer it, letting the excess marinade drip off, to a plate. Discard the marinade.

5. Remove the baking sheet from the oven and turn the oven to broil. Push the veggies to the outer edges of the pan, then add the steak to the center. Return the baking sheet to the oven and broil for 5 minutes, then flip the steak, stir the veggies, and cook 6 minutes more for medium-rare. Remove the steak from the baking sheet and let it rest on a cutting board for 5 to 10 minutes.

6. **Meanwhile, make the chimichurri.** In a medium bowl, stir together the cilantro, mango, Fresno pepper, vinegar, olive oil, and lime juice. Add the avocado and gently toss to combine.

7. To serve, slice the steak against the grain and top with the chimichurri. Store any leftovers refrigerated in an airtight container for up to 3 days.

BEEF BOURGUIGNON

SERVES: 6

PREP TIME: 15 minutes
COOK TIME: 55 minutes, plus additional
time to come to pressure
TOTAL TIME: 1 hour 10 minutes

If there was ever a recipe to call magic, it's this beef bourguignon—a traditional French stew that's meant to be slowly simmered in red wine (often burgundy) for hours and hours and hours until the meat is tender and melts in your mouth. It's a classic recipe, made famous in America by Julia Child, and if you've ever made it, you know it's always impressive. But let's be real, some of us are not as organized as we might like to be. Sometimes we need to make a fancy dinner, but without taking up a lot of time. Here is where your pressure cooker saves the day. It cuts the cooking time down to just an hour but yields the same melt-in-your-mouth beef stew that everyone loves . . . just like magic. Serve this with buttery mashed potatoes and crusty no-knead bread (see page 20) for a dinner that everyone will walk away raving about.

2 pounds beef chuck (fat trimmed away), cubed

2 tablespoons all-purpose flour

Kosher salt and freshly ground pepper

4 slices thick-cut bacon, chopped

1 medium yellow onion, diced

2 garlic cloves, minced or grated

4 carrots, sliced

1 cup sliced cremini mushrooms

2 cups dry red wine, such as Pinot Noir

1 cup low-sodium beef broth

2 tablespoons tomato paste

4 sprigs of fresh thyme

The Best Pressure Cooker Mashed Potatoes (page 62) or store-bought mashed potatoes

1. In a large bowl, combine the beef, flour, and a pinch each of salt and pepper. Toss to coat.

2. Scatter the bacon into the pressure cooker pot and, using the sauté function, cook, stirring frequently, until the fat has rendered and the bacon is crispy, about 5 minutes. Remove the bacon from the pot and drain on a paper towel–lined plate. Discard all but 1 tablespoon of the bacon grease.

3. Add the beef to the pot and, using the sauté function, cook until browned on all sides, about 5 minutes. Stir in the onion, garlic, carrots, mushrooms, and a pinch each of salt and pepper. Pour in the wine and beef broth, then add the tomato paste, thyme, and bacon. Stir to combine. Lock the lid in place, select high pressure, and cook for 35 minutes.

4. Quick or natural release, then open when the pressure subsides. Remove the thyme sprigs and discard. Using the sauté function, cook until the sauce has thickened slightly, about 10 minutes more.

5. Serve the beef over mashed potatoes.

6. Store any leftovers refrigerated in an airtight container for up to 3 days.

BEEF & LAMB   209

POMEGRANATE-BRAISED
SHORT RIBS
WITH SWEET POTATO MASH

SERVES: 6

PREP TIME: 20 minutes
COOK TIME: 5 to 8 hours

As if you couldn't tell, I love an all-in-one dinner. Skillet chicken and potatoes? Check. One-pan pasta and meatballs? Yup. Next up, slow cooker short ribs and sweet potatoes. As you're putting this dish together you may worry that there's a lot of stuff going into your slow cooker and that it might not all fit. You might be tempted to doubt my method, but don't. Everything fits nice and snugly. And as the slow cooker works its magic, the onions melt down, the short ribs become tender, and the sweet potatoes become soft. By the end of cooking, you'll have a heavenly dinner—a complete meal—that required very little effort. The best!

2 tablespoons extra-virgin olive oil

5 pounds beef short ribs

Kosher salt and freshly ground pepper

1 medium yellow onion, thinly sliced

2 shallots, thinly sliced

1 tablespoon honey

1½ cups pomegranate juice

1 (1-inch) piece of fresh ginger, peeled and grated

2 sprigs of fresh thyme, plus 1 tablespoon chopped fresh thyme

3 medium sweet potatoes

4 tablespoons salted butter

Seeds from 1 pomegranate

1. Heat the olive oil in a large skillet over high heat. Season the short ribs with salt and pepper. When the oil shimmers, add the ribs and sear until browned, about 3 minutes per side. Transfer the ribs to the slow cooker pot.

2. Arrange the onion and shallots around the ribs in the slow cooker pot and drizzle the honey over them. Add the pomegranate juice, ginger, and thyme sprigs. Prick the sweet potatoes all over with a fork and place them on top of the ribs. Cover and cook until the meat is tender and falling off the bone, 7 to 8 hours on low, or 5 to 6 hours on high.

3. Remove the potatoes and set aside to cool slightly.

4. Meanwhile, skim off any fat that has collected on top of the slow cooker pot (see Note).

5. In a small skillet, melt the butter over medium heat until just browned, 3 to 5 minutes. Stir in the chopped thyme, then remove the skillet from the heat.

6. Peel the sweet potatoes, if desired. Place in a medium bowl and mash. Add the browned butter and mash with the sweet potatoes until combined. Taste and add salt and pepper as needed.

7. Divide the sweet potatoes among six plates and top each with ribs and pomegranate seeds. Spoon the sauce over the ribs to serve.

8. Store any leftovers refrigerated in an airtight container for up to 3 days.

. . . .

After skimming the fat from the slow cooker, you can remove and discard the short rib bones and use two forks to lightly shred the meat, if you like.

THAI BASIL BEEF

WITH PEANUT SALSA

SERVES: 4

PREP TIME: 5 minutes
COOK TIME: 15 minutes
TOTAL TIME: 20 minutes

When it comes to packing in flavor, sweet Thai chili sauce is probably my favorite store-bought sauce. It makes almost any dish better, but I especially love using it to make a super-quick Thai-style beef. Serve this over rice noodles and you'll have dinner on the table in less than thirty minutes. Also, I don't know if "peanut salsa" is actually a thing, but it is for me, and it's probably one of my better ideas ever. If you're skeptical, I get it, but don't knock it till you try it. It's delightful atop this Thai basil beef.

8 ounces rice noodles

2 tablespoons sesame oil

1 pound lean ground beef

3 garlic cloves, minced or grated

1 (1-inch) piece of fresh ginger, peeled and grated

½ cup Thai sweet chili sauce

¼ cup low-sodium soy sauce

1 cup fresh basil leaves, chopped, plus more for serving

Juice of 2 limes

½ cup salted peanuts, chopped

1 red Fresno pepper, seeded and chopped

3 carrots, shaved into ribbons

2 green onions, thinly sliced

Fresh mint leaves, for serving (optional)

1. Bring a large saucepan of water to a boil over high heat. Add the rice noodles and cook according to the package directions, until softened.

2. **Make the sauce.** In a large skillet, heat the sesame oil over medium heat. When the oil shimmers, add the beef and cook, breaking up the beef with a wooden spoon, until browned, 5 to 8 minutes. Add the garlic and ginger and cook until fragrant, about 1 minute more. Stir in the sweet chili sauce, soy sauce, and ½ cup of water and cook until the sauce thickens slightly, about 5 minutes. Add the rice noodles and cook, tossing to coat, until warmed through, about 1 minute. Remove the skillet from the heat and stir in the basil and half of the lime juice.

3. **Make the salsa.** In a small bowl, stir together the peanuts, the remaining lime juice, and the Fresno pepper.

4. Divide the noodles among four bowls and top each with peanut salsa, carrots, green onions, and mint, if desired.

KOREAN BEEF

WITH YUM YUM SAUCE

SERVES: 6

PREP TIME: 15 minutes
COOK TIME: 20 minutes
TOTAL TIME: 35 minutes

If you've been following along with me for a while now, you may remember when my younger brother Red won a gold medal for snowboarding at the 2018 Winter Olympics in South Korea. The medal was cool and all, but the Korean beef was better. Just kidding . . . kind of. In all seriousness, if you've ever had real-deal Korean-style beef, you know it's one of the most delicious explosions of flavor your mouth will ever experience. As soon as I returned home from that trip, I cooked this dish. And then I made it over and over again until I got the flavors just right and it tasted as authentic as I was ever going to be able to make it. The most important ingredient is gochujang, or Korean chili paste. Look for it in your local grocery store's Asian aisle, or do as I do and order it online.

½ cup low-sodium soy sauce

2 tablespoons honey

1 to 2 tablespoons gochujang

1 (1-inch) piece of fresh ginger, peeled and grated

2 garlic cloves, grated

2 teaspoons toasted sesame oil, plus more for serving

2 tablespoons extra-virgin olive oil, sesame oil, or peanut oil

2 cups sliced cremini or wild mushrooms

4 cups baby spinach

1½ pounds skirt or flank steak, thinly sliced against the grain

4 green onions, thinly sliced

⅓ cup fresh basil leaves, roughly chopped

3 cups steamed rice, for serving

2 tablespoons toasted sesame seeds, for garnish

2 carrots, shaved into ribbons

Yum Yum Sauce (recipe follows) or store-bought, such as Terry Ho's Yum Yum Sauce, for serving

1. In a small bowl or glass measuring cup, whisk together the soy sauce, honey, gochujang, ginger, garlic, and sesame oil.

2. In a large skillet, heat 1 tablespoon of the olive oil over high heat. When the oil shimmers, add the mushrooms and cook until softened, about 3 minutes. Add the spinach and cook until wilted, about 2 minutes more. Transfer the veggies to a plate.

3. In the same skillet, heat the remaining 1 tablespoon of olive oil over high heat. When the oil shimmers, add the steak and sear, tossing once during cooking, until the edges are caramelized, 5 to 8 minutes. Pour in the soy sauce mixture and bring to a boil. Reduce the heat to medium and cook until the sauce thickens, about 5 minutes. Add the green onions and cook until wilted, about 1 minute more. Remove the skillet from the heat and stir in the basil.

4. Divide the rice among six bowls and spoon the veggies over the top. Add the beef and garnish with toasted sesame seeds and carrots. Serve the yum yum sauce alongside for dipping.

5. Store any leftovers refrigerated in an airtight container for up to 3 days.

 <10

YUM YUM SAUCE

～ MAKES: ¾ cup ～

½ cup tahini

1 teaspoon honey

1 teaspoon smoked paprika

1 teaspoon garlic powder

1 teaspoon onion powder

½ teaspoon chili powder

Kosher salt

In a small bowl, combine the tahini, honey, paprika, garlic powder, onion powder, chili powder, salt, and ⅓ cup of water and whisk until smooth. Store refrigerated in an airtight container for up to 2 weeks.

DRY-RUBBED GRILLED STEAK

WITH GARLIC-BUTTER CORN SALAD

. . . .
SERVES: 6
. . . .

PREP TIME: 20 minutes
COOK TIME: 20 minutes
TOTAL TIME: 40 minutes

This recipe is literally a summer BBQ on a plate. The steak is seasoned with my favorite homemade dry spice rub. You grill it until it's charred on the outside and tender and juicy inside. And then there's the garlic butter corn salad. Oh, wow! Be sure to spoon it over your steak—steak topped with salad makes every single bite delicious. Trust me, do not miss out—I promise this salad is amazing. This is the quickest of dinners, the simplest of dinners, and also one of the best. Enough said.

DRY-RUBBED STEAK

1 tablespoon smoked paprika

2 teaspoons kosher salt

2 teaspoons freshly ground pepper

1 teaspoon onion powder

1 teaspoon garlic powder

½ teaspoon ground cayenne pepper

2 pounds skirt or flank steak

GARLIC-BUTTER CORN SALAD

2 tablespoons salted butter

3 cups fresh raw corn kernels (cut from about 4 ears of corn)

2 garlic cloves, minced or grated

1 tablespoon fresh thyme leaves

2 green onions, sliced

1 jalapeño pepper, seeded and chopped

Kosher salt and freshly ground pepper

1 cup cherry tomatoes, halved

Juice of 1 lemon

Juice of 1 lime

⅓ cup fresh basil leaves, roughly torn

1. **Make the steak.** In a small bowl, stir together the smoked paprika, salt, pepper, onion powder, garlic powder, and cayenne. Rub the spice mixture all over the steak.

2. Heat a grill to high or a grill pan over high heat. When the grill is just smoking, add the steak. Grill for 5 to 8 minutes, then flip and cook about 5 minutes more for medium-rare. Transfer the steak to a cutting board and let rest for 10 minutes.

3. **Meanwhile, make the salad.** Melt the butter in a large skillet over medium heat. Add 2 cups of the corn, the garlic, thyme, green onions, jalapeño, and a pinch each of salt and pepper. Cook until the corn is caramelized, about 5 minutes. Remove the skillet from the heat and stir in the remaining 1 cup of corn and the tomatoes, lemon juice, lime juice, and basil.

4. Slice the steak thinly against the grain. Serve topped with corn salad.

5. Store any leftovers refrigerated in an airtight container for up to 3 days.

BAKED COCONUT-CURRY MEATBALLS

SERVES: 6

PREP TIME: 20 minutes
COOK TIME: 25 minutes
TOTAL TIME: 45 minutes

Lamb curry is something you might not think to make at home. But transforming the dish into a quick-cooking meatball curry makes it approachable any night of the week. By using ground meat, you cut down on the cooking time and can have this dish ready to eat in thirty minutes or less. I always bake meatballs in the oven, as opposed to pan-frying them. I don't know about you, but I have zero interest in standing at the stove and tending to meatballs for half an hour. No thanks! Plus, I've also found that baking helps meatballs hold their shape and keeps them from drying out. This curry is extra saucy, so serve it over couscous or rice and with fresh naan for dipping.

1 pound lean ground beef or lamb

2 tablespoons full-fat plain Greek yogurt

2 green onions, chopped

1½ teaspoons chipotle chile powder

Kosher salt and freshly ground pepper

2 tablespoons extra-virgin olive oil

1 small yellow onion, chopped

4 garlic cloves, minced or grated

1 (1-inch) piece of fresh ginger, peeled and grated

1 tablespoon yellow curry powder

½ teaspoon ground cinnamon

1 (14-ounce) can full-fat unsweetened coconut milk

Juice of 1 lemon

⅓ cup fresh cilantro, roughly chopped

Steamed white or brown rice, for serving

Naan, for serving

1. Preheat the oven to 450°F. Line a rimmed baking sheet with parchment paper.

2. **Make the meatballs.** In a medium bowl, place the ground beef, yogurt, green onions, ½ teaspoon of the chipotle chile powder, and a pinch each of salt and pepper. Using your hands, mix well until combined. Grease your hands with a bit of olive oil and roll the mixture into fifteen to twenty 2-tablespoon-size balls. Place the meatballs on the prepared baking sheet and bake until they are crisp on the outside and cooked through, about 15 minutes.

3. **Meanwhile, make the sauce.** Heat the olive oil in a large skillet over medium heat. When the oil shimmers, add the onion and cook until softened, about 5 minutes. Add the garlic and ginger and cook until fragrant, about 5 minutes more. Stir in the remaining 1 teaspoon of chile powder, the curry powder, and the cinnamon and cook until fragrant, about 1 minute. Stir in the coconut milk and ½ cup of water, increase the heat to medium-high, and bring the sauce to a boil. Cook until the sauce thickens slightly, about 5 minutes. Stir in the lemon juice.

4. Add the meatballs and cook, stirring occasionally, until the sauce thickens further, about 5 minutes more. Remove the skillet from the heat and stir in the cilantro.

5. Serve the meatballs and sauce with rice and naan.

6. Store any leftovers refrigerated in an airtight container for up to 3 days.

SEAFOOD &
FISH

LEMONY HALIBUT AND CHICKPEAS

WITH FARRO

SERVES: 4

PREP TIME: 15 minutes
COOK TIME: 15 minutes
TOTAL TIME: 30 minutes

This recipe is going to surprise you. It might look like a sheet pan full of health, but don't be fooled. While this halibut is admittedly fresh and healthy, it's also hearty, packed with flavor, and so satisfying. Not to mention you get protein, carbs, *and* veggies all in one dish. Seasoning the halibut with a dash or two of smoked paprika is the key to giving it flavor, while using Meyer lemon makes everything especially citrusy. If you happen to have leftovers, it makes a great lunch salad the following day.

4 (8-ounce) halibut fillets

5 tablespoons extra-virgin olive oil

½ teaspoon smoked paprika

1 tablespoon fresh thyme leaves

Crushed red pepper flakes

Kosher salt and freshly ground pepper

1 Honeycrisp apple, cored and sliced

1 medium yellow onion, cut into 8 wedges

1 (14-ounce) can chickpeas, drained, rinsed, and patted dry

1 Meyer or regular lemon, sliced

3 sprigs of fresh thyme

1½ cups cooked farro or quinoa (see Note)

1 bunch of Tuscan kale, stemmed and roughly chopped

2 tablespoons balsamic vinegar

1. Preheat the oven to 450°F.

2. Rub the halibut all over with 1 tablespoon of the olive oil, the paprika, thyme leaves, red pepper flakes, and a pinch each of salt and pepper. Place on a rimmed baking sheet. Arrange the apple, onion, and chickpeas around the fish and drizzle 2 tablespoons of the olive oil over them. Season with salt and pepper. Arrange the lemon slices and thyme sprigs on top of the apple and onion. Bake until the halibut is opaque and flakes easily, 11 to 14 minutes. Turn the oven to broil and cook until the fish is lightly charred, about 1 minute more. Remove the baking sheet from the oven, reduce the oven temperature to 400°F, and transfer the halibut to a plate.

3. Add the farro and kale to the baking sheet with the apple and onion and drizzle with the remaining 2 tablespoons of olive oil and the vinegar. Toss to combine. Return the halibut to the baking sheet and place it back in the oven to cook until warmed through, 3 to 5 minutes more. Serve warm.

Cook a large batch of farro or quinoa over the weekend to quickly make this recipe on busy weeknights.

JALAPEÑO GARLIC-BUTTER SHRIMP

SERVES: 4

PREP TIME: 10 minutes
COOK TIME: 10 minutes
TOTAL TIME: 20 minutes, plus 15 minutes to marinate

My brother Trevor and I are known as the "terrible Ts" of the family. Why? Because we're a pain, we're stubborn, and we usually get what we want. Yes, it's true. Well, Trev is a huge fan of Hawaiian food, and it's thanks to him that I first discovered Hawaiian-style shrimp. My version is more of a sweet-and-spicy take, with a mix of fresh jalapeños, mangoes, and both lemon and lime. And, yes, of course some butter, too, because butter and shrimp go together like peanut butter and jelly; they need each other. This may not be traditional, but it sure is good. Perfect for busy weeknights when you're looking for something a little more special but still quick and satisfying.

1 pound large, raw tail-on shrimp, peeled and deveined

4 tablespoons extra-virgin olive oil

2 tablespoons honey

4 to 6 garlic cloves, finely chopped

2 jalapeño peppers, seeded and chopped

Juice of 1 lime

Juice of 1 lemon

4 tablespoons salted butter

Kosher salt and freshly ground pepper

¼ cup fresh cilantro, chopped

1. In a large zip-top bag, combine the shrimp, 3 tablespoons of the olive oil, the honey, garlic, jalapeños, lime juice, and lemon juice. Turn to coat. Marinate in the fridge for 15 to 30 minutes.

2. In a large skillet, heat the remaining 1 tablespoon of olive oil over medium heat. When the oil shimmers, use a slotted spoon to scoop the shrimp and garlic out of the marinade, reserving it, and transfer them to the skillet. Cook until the shrimp are pink, about 2 minutes per side. Add the reserved marinade, butter, and a pinch each of salt and pepper. Continue cooking until the garlic turns light golden brown, 1 to 2 minutes more. Remove the skillet from the heat and stir in the cilantro.

Serve this shrimp over rice or stuff into tacos and finish it off with your favorite slaw.

PARCHMENT-BAKED
GREEK SALMON AND ZUCCHINI
WITH SALTY FETA

SERVES: 4

PREP TIME: 15 minutes
COOK TIME: 20 minutes
TOTAL TIME: 35 minutes

For how quick, easy, flavorful, healthy, and delicious this recipe is, you'd never guess that it requires only one sheet pan, parchment paper, and less than forty minutes of your time (most of which is hands-off!). A parchment packet is an Italian way of cooking fish. To put it simply, you're cooking your food inside a packet made from parchment paper. Not only does it save on mess and dishes, but this method steams the food and cooks everything in its own juices. Cooking the salmon this way preserves nutrients and creates an insane amount of flavor, because all the aromas are trapped inside the parchment paper. Meaning you can get away with using fewer ingredients but still come away with a delicious dinner. Another great thing about this recipe is that it's an all-in-one dinner, complete with protein, carbs, and veggies.

¼ cup extra-virgin olive oil

2 garlic cloves, minced or grated

Juice of 1 lemon

1 tablespoon chopped fresh dill

2 teaspoons smoked paprika

Kosher salt and freshly ground pepper

1 small russet potato, very thinly sliced into ¼-inch rounds

1 small zucchini, thinly sliced

4 (6- to 8-ounce) salmon fillets, skin removed

1 lemon, sliced

⅓ cup pitted kalamata olives

4 ounces feta cheese, crumbled

Crushed red pepper flakes

Fresh arugula and basil, for serving

1. Preheat the oven to 400°F.

2. In a small bowl, combine the olive oil, garlic, lemon juice, dill, smoked paprika, and a pinch each of salt and pepper.

3. Open the parchment packets and lay them flat on a clean work surface. On one half of one packet, arrange one-fourth of the potato slices in an even layer (about the size of your piece of fish) and season with salt and pepper. Layer one-fourth of the zucchini on top of the potato and season with salt and pepper. Place one salmon fillet on top of the zucchini, drizzle with the olive oil mixture, and top with 2 lemon slices. Scatter a few olives around the fish. Repeat with the remaining parchment and ingredients.

4. To seal the packets, fold the bare half of the parchment over the salmon and fold in the open edges twice. Place the packets on a rimmed baking sheet. Bake until the potatoes are tender, 18 to 20 minutes.

5. Remove the baking sheet from the oven. Transfer the packets to plates and open carefully, tearing away and discarding the top half of the paper. Serve with crumbled feta, red pepper flakes, and fresh arugula and basil on top.

You can cut large (15 × 16-inch) pieces of parchment paper and fold them in half to make your own packets, or you can now find pre-made parchment packets at some stores, meant for recipes just like this. I buy mine online . . . where I buy everything.

LOBSTER TACOS

WITH CHARRED POBLANO CREMA

SERVES: 4

PREP TIME: 15 minutes
COOK TIME: 15 minutes
TOTAL TIME: 30 minutes

Lobsters are almost always considered a treat—maybe because they're regional or maybe because it takes a lot of work to get to all that delicious meat. My trick to make cooking lobster faster and simpler: just use the tails. Tails are much easier to work with than most of the rest of the lobster and often contain the most desired meat anyway. I pan-sear the tails, pull out the meat, then serve it inside charred tortillas. Salsa and a quick-roasted poblano pepper crema really seal the deal. And, yes, there is also cheese here, which I know is controversial, but I don't tend to follow rules all that well—especially not in the kitchen. You can take or leave the cheese, but if I were you, I'd take it. I've created a bit of a cheesy quesadilla taco shell, and it's just as crazy delicious as it sounds.

POBLANO CREMA

1 poblano pepper

1 cup full-fat plain Greek yogurt

Juice of 1 lime

Kosher salt

LOBSTER TACOS

4 lobster tails, halved lengthwise (see Note)

2 tablespoons extra-virgin olive oil

1 cup shredded fontina cheese

12 to 16 corn tortillas, warmed

Mango Salsa (recipe follows) or store-bought salsa, for serving

1 avocado, sliced, for serving

1. **Make the crema.** Turn one stove burner to high heat. Using heat-proof tongs, carefully place the poblano directly over the flame and char, turning until blackened all over, 3 to 5 minutes. Transfer the poblano to a medium bowl and cover with a plate. Let it steam, about 10 minutes, then remove and discard the charred skin, stem, and seeds.

2. Add the poblano, yogurt, lime juice, 2 tablespoons of water, and a pinch of salt to a blender or food processor and pulse until smooth, about 30 seconds, adding water 1 tablespoon at a time, as needed, to thin.

3. **Make the tacos.** Heat a large skillet over medium-high heat. Rub each lobster tail with olive oil and place them cut side down in the skillet. Cook until lightly golden, 3 to 5 minutes, then flip and continue cooking until the shells turn bright red, about 5 minutes more. Remove the tails from the skillet. Let sit until cool enough to handle, then remove and discard the shells. Roughly chop the meat.

4. To assemble the tacos, divide the cheese among half of the warmed tortillas, then top each with a remaining tortilla (as though you're making a quesadilla). Fold the cheese-stuffed tortillas into a taco shape and add the lobster, salsa, and avocado. Drizzle with poblano crema.

<10

MANGO SALSA

~ MAKES: about 1½ cups ~

1 mango, peeled and chopped

1 cup yellow cherry tomatoes, halved

1 jalapeño pepper, seeded and chopped

¼ cup fresh cilantro, chopped

Juice of 1 lime

Kosher salt

In a small bowl, stir together the mango, tomatoes, jalapeño, cilantro, lime juice, and a pinch of salt. Store refrigerated in an airtight container for up to 2 days.

You'll know your lobster is done when the shells turn a fiery red color and the meat is opaque. Tails cook through quickly, so watch them closely.

I cut my lobster tails in half lengthwise using a sharp chef's knife. If you would prefer not to do this, just ask your butcher or fishmonger to do so for you.

EXTRA-SAUCY COCONUT FISH CURRY

WITH POMEGRANATE

SERVES: 4

PREP TIME: 15 minutes
COOK TIME: 15 minutes
TOTAL TIME: 30 minutes

Cod is a sort of bland, white fish I've always found a little boring. Here's what I have learned, though. Cod's mellow nature means it can be used in dishes with a super-flavorful sauce—the fish takes on the taste of whatever you're serving it with. That said, I am pleased to introduce this coconut fish curry. It's quick cooking, healthy, and colorful, and each bowl is finished with toasted coconut . . . an unexpected but *oh-so-good* twist.

2 tablespoons coconut oil

½ medium yellow onion, chopped

2 tablespoons red curry paste

2 tablespoons finely chopped fresh lemongrass

1 (1-inch) piece of fresh ginger, peeled and grated

1 (14-ounce) can full-fat unsweetened coconut milk

2 tablespoons fish sauce

1 pound fresh or frozen cod fillets, thawed if frozen, cut into 1-inch pieces (see Note)

Zest and juice of 1 lime

¼ cup fresh cilantro, chopped

3 cups cooked rice

Seeds from 1 pomegranate, for garnish

½ cup toasted unsweetened flaked coconut, for garnish

1. Melt the coconut oil in a large skillet over high heat. Add the onion and cook, stirring, until softened, about 5 minutes. Stir in the curry paste, lemongrass, and ginger and cook until fragrant, about 1 minute more.

2. Stir in the coconut milk and fish sauce and bring the mixture to a boil. Add the cod and reduce the heat to medium. Cook until the fish is opaque and flakes easily, 5 to 8 minutes more. Remove the skillet from the heat and stir in the lime zest, lime juice, and cilantro.

3. To serve, divide the rice among four bowls and spoon the curry over the top. Garnish with pomegranate seeds and toasted coconut.

. . . .

Any other white fish, such as halibut or tilapia, would also work nicely. You could even use peeled and deveined shrimp.

SLOW-ROASTED MOROCCAN SALMON

WITH WINTER SQUASH

SERVES: 6

PREP TIME: 15 minutes
COOK TIME: 40 minutes
TOTAL TIME: 55 minutes

If I had to choose only one salmon recipe to make for eternity, this would be it. Or at least that's how I feel at this very moment. The point I'm trying to make is that I really love this recipe. It has all my favorite flavors, shows off my favorite autumn and winter produce, is incredibly easy, beautiful, and just really dang delicious. I'll often make this for a dinner when friends come over, but it's really great for any occasion. Serve it with steamed couscous for a truly Moroccan-inspired dinner.

1 acorn squash, sliced into half-moons

2 tablespoons plus ⅓ cup extra-virgin olive oil

3 tablespoons honey

1 tablespoon sambal oelek (garlic chili paste)

Kosher salt

1 (2-pound) salmon fillet

1 tablespoon harissa seasoning

3 garlic cloves, smashed

1 Meyer lemon, sliced

Seeds from 1 pomegranate

Fresh mint or cilantro, for serving

1. Preheat the oven to 425°F. Line a rimmed baking sheet with parchment paper.

2. On the rimmed baking sheet, combine the squash, 2 tablespoons of the olive oil, the honey, sambal oelek, and a generous pinch of salt. Toss to coat and arrange the squash in an even layer. Bake until the squash is tender, about 15 minutes. Remove the baking sheet from the oven and reduce the temperature to 325°F.

3. Push the squash to the outer edges of the pan. Place the salmon in the center, rub the top with harissa, and season with salt. Scatter the garlic and lemon slices around the salmon and pour the remaining ⅓ cup of olive oil over everything. Return the baking sheet to the oven and roast until the salmon is opaque and flakes easily, 20 to 30 minutes.

4. Transfer the salmon and squash to six plates. Top with pomegranate seeds and fresh mint to serve.

This recipe calls for harissa seasoning, which is different from harissa paste. Harissa seasoning is a spice blend and can be found in the spice aisle at most grocery stores; otherwise look online.

BROWNED-BUTTER SCALLOPS

WITH BURST CHERRY TOMATOES

SERVES: 4

PREP TIME: 10 minutes
COOK TIME: 20 minutes
TOTAL TIME: 30 minutes

Is there anything better than extra-buttery scallops? Yes, there is, and it's called *browned*-butter scallops. I might be a bit dramatic here, but browned butter really takes things up a level . . . or three. Its nutty, toasted flavor makes for rich scallops that melt in your mouth. I've paired these with a cherry tomato pan sauce that makes this recipe ideal for summer, but that is still great throughout the year, as cherry tomatoes are available in every season. For a quick and easy dinner, spoon the scallops over pasta. Or serve them as an appetizer with crusty bread, perfect for soaking up all that delicious sauciness.

4 tablespoons extra-virgin olive oil

1 pound large scallops

Kosher salt and freshly ground pepper

4 garlic cloves, smashed

1 tablespoon chopped fresh thyme

Crushed red pepper flakes

4 tablespoons salted butter

¼ cup dry white wine, such as pinot grigio or Sauvignon Blanc

2 cups cherry tomatoes

2 chives, chopped

Zest of 1 lemon

1. In a large skillet, heat 2 tablespoons of the olive oil over medium heat. Season the scallops with salt and pepper on both sides. When the oil shimmers, add the scallops and sear until browned, 2 to 3 minutes per side. Transfer the scallops to a plate.

2. In the same skillet, combine the remaining 2 tablespoons of olive oil and the garlic, thyme, and a pinch of red pepper flakes. Cook until fragrant, 3 to 4 minutes. Add the butter and cook, stirring occasionally, until just browned, 2 to 3 minutes more. Slowly pour in the wine, then add the tomatoes and cook until the tomatoes burst and the wine has reduced slightly, about 5 minutes.

3. Return the scallops and any collected juices to the skillet and cook until warmed through, about 3 minutes. Remove the skillet from the heat.

4. Serve the scallops with the tomatoes and spoon the pan sauce over the top. Finish with chives and lemon zest.

JERK SHRIMP AND MANGO SALSA RICE BOWLS

SERVES: 4

PREP TIME: 25 minutes
COOK TIME: 10 minutes
TOTAL TIME: 35 minutes

One of my favorite vacation destinations is the Caribbean. Clear blue waters, white sandy beaches, palm trees, fresh fruit, and jerk dishes always keep me longing for a reunion. There is just so much flavor in Caribbean food. While it might not be a super-authentic version, this recipe is my take on jerk shrimp. It's a mash-up of Caribbean and Mexican flavors, with spicy shrimp and a sweet mango salsa. I make this whenever I need to mentally escape the frozen tundra I call home and drift into a more tropical mind-set. It's obviously not the same as being seaside in the Caribbean, but it's a nice compromise for those of us who can't hop on a jet for the weekend.

1½ pounds small shrimp, peeled and deveined

2 tablespoons extra-virgin olive oil

2 tablespoons The Best Jerk Seasoning (recipe follows) or store-bought blend

4 medium to large tomatillos, husked and halved

1 jalapeño pepper, seeded

Juice of 1 lime

¼ cup fresh cilantro, chopped

1 mango, peeled and diced

Kosher salt

3 cups cooked rice

1 (14-ounce) can black beans, drained and rinsed

2 green onions, chopped, for serving

1 avocado, sliced, for serving

1. Preheat the oven to 425°F.

2. On a rimmed baking sheet, combine the shrimp, olive oil, and jerk seasoning and toss to coat. Arrange in an even layer on half of the baking sheet. On the other half of the sheet, place the tomatillos and jalapeño, spacing them apart. Roast until the shrimp are pink and cooked through and the tomatillos are lightly charred, about 10 minutes.

3. In a blender or food processor, combine the roasted tomatillos and jalapeño, lime juice, and cilantro and blend until smooth. Stir in the mango and a pinch of salt.

4. In a large bowl, stir together the rice and black beans.

5. Divide the rice and beans among four bowls. Add the shrimp and top each dish with the tomatillo salsa, green onions, and avocado.

<10

THE BEST JERK SEASONING

~ MAKES: ½ cup ~

⅓ cup smoked paprika

1 tablespoon ground allspice

1 tablespoon chipotle chile powder

1 tablespoon dried thyme

1 teaspoon garlic powder

1 teaspoon ground cinnamon

1 to 2 teaspoons ground cayenne pepper

2 teaspoons kosher salt

2 teaspoons freshly ground pepper

Combine the paprika, allspice, chile powder, thyme, garlic powder, cinnamon, cayenne, salt, and pepper. Transfer to a glass jar or other airtight container and store in a cool, dry place for up to 3 months.

CLAMS ON TOAST
IN HERBED WHITE WINE

SERVES: 2

PREP TIME: 15 minutes
COOK TIME: 15 minutes
TOTAL TIME: 30 minutes

I really like cooking with wine. When it comes to making sauces, it's a total flavor booster. I especially love the combination of clams and white wine—it's delicate and pairs nicely with the salty prosciutto and fresh herbs in this recipe. And, yes, I realize this is a very fancy way to enjoy toast, but I am okay with that. In fact, I think it works just perfectly. I like this dish best for dinner, when I'm feeling like something fancy and "grown up" but still want it to be easy. Also, even though *I* love the wine in this recipe, I understand that some of you may prefer not to cook with wine. It's okay: I get it. If this is the case for you, simply substitute chicken broth.

2 tablespoons extra-virgin olive oil, plus more for serving

4 slices thick-cut sourdough bread

4 garlic cloves, 2 halved, 2 smashed

3 ounces thinly sliced prosciutto, torn

2 tablespoons fresh thyme leaves

1 tablespoon chopped fresh oregano

1 cup dry white wine, such as pinot grigio or Sauvignon Blanc

Kosher salt and freshly ground pepper

2 pounds Manila clams (see Note)

Crushed red pepper flakes, for serving

Fresh basil leaves, for serving

1. In a large skillet, heat the olive oil over medium heat. When the oil shimmers, add the bread and cook until golden and toasted, 1 to 2 minutes per side. Remove the bread from the skillet and rub each piece with the cut side of one of the halved garlic cloves.

2. Using the same skillet, cook the prosciutto over medium heat, without moving it, until crisp, 2 to 3 minutes per side. Remove the prosciutto and set aside. Add the smashed garlic, thyme, and oregano and cook until fragrant, about 1 minute. Pour in the wine, season with salt and pepper, and bring to a simmer over high heat. Add the clams and cook until the clams open and the sauce reduces by one-third, 8 to 10 minutes. Discard any clams that do not open after 10 minutes.

3. To serve, divide the toast between two plates and spoon the clams and wine sauce over the top. Crumble the prosciutto over the clams. Top with red pepper flakes and fresh basil. Store any leftover sauce refrigerated in an airtight container for 1 to 2 days.

Try to find Manila clams, which are smaller and better suited for this recipe. If you're using littleneck clams, you might need to cook them about 5 minutes longer than indicated to get them to open up.

HERBY LOBSTER

TAGLIATELLE

....

SERVES: 6

....

PREP TIME: 10 minutes
COOK TIME: 20 minutes
TOTAL TIME: 30 minutes

During my very first year writing *Half Baked Harvest*, I made homemade lobster ravioli in a creamy tomato sauce. If you type "lobster ravioli" into the search bar on my website, it will pop up. The photos make me cringe, and the recipe needs to be edited, but it's still one of the most mouthwatering seafood recipes I have on the blog. It's also one of the more difficult recipes, but, shockingly, a relatively popular one. Well, longtime readers, rejoice: this is my easier version of lobster pasta. It's not ravioli, but it's just as good and takes only a quarter of the time to prepare. One of my tricks is boiling the lobster and pasta in the same pot of water. (Saves time and dishes!) To keep the pasta rich like the original recipe, I added some burrata cheese. Oh, and don't even think about skipping those lemony, toasted torn bread chunks—they pull this dish together, adding a perfect little crunch to every bite.

4 tablespoons extra-virgin olive oil

1 cup torn ciabatta bread

Kosher salt

Zest of 1 lemon

4 lobster tails, scrubbed clean and halved lengthwise

1 (1-pound box) tagliatelle pasta

2 tablespoons salted butter

3 cups cherry tomatoes

4 garlic cloves, smashed

1 teaspoon crushed red pepper flakes

2 tablespoons fresh thyme leaves

1 tablespoon chopped fresh dill, plus more for serving

Freshly ground pepper

1 large handful of fresh basil leaves, roughly chopped, plus more for serving

2 balls of fresh burrata cheese, torn (optional)

1. In a large skillet, heat 2 tablespoons of the olive oil over medium heat. When the oil shimmers, add the bread pieces and a pinch of salt. Cook, stirring occasionally, until golden and toasted all over, about 5 minutes. Remove the skillet from the heat and stir in the lemon zest. Transfer the torn bread to a plate and set aside. Wipe the skillet clean.

2. Meanwhile, bring a large pot of salted water to a boil. Add the lobster tails and cook until the shells turn bright red, about 5 minutes. Using tongs, carefully remove the tails from the water. Add the pasta to the boiling water and cook according to the package directions, until al dente. Reserve 1 cup of the pasta cooking water and drain the rest.

3. Once the tails are cool enough to handle, remove and discard the shells. Roughly chop the reserved meat.

4. Meanwhile, heat the remaining 2 tablespoons of olive oil and the butter together in the cleaned skillet. When the oil shimmers, add the tomatoes, garlic, red pepper flakes, thyme, dill, and a pinch each of salt and pepper and cook until the tomatoes begin to pop, 4 to 5 minutes. Add the lobster meat, pasta, and ⅓ cup of the pasta cooking water. Toss to combine. Remove the skillet from the heat and stir in the basil. If necessary, add more pasta cooking water, 1 tablespoon at a time, until your desired consistency is reached.

5. Remove and discard the garlic cloves. Divide the pasta among six bowls and top each with torn burrata (if desired), torn bread, dill, and basil.

LEMON BUTTER COD

WITH ORZO AND ASPARAGUS

SERVES: 4

PREP TIME: 10 minutes
COOK TIME: 20 minutes
TOTAL TIME: 30 minutes

My dad has instilled in me a serious love of saucy food. The more spices, herbs, and, yes, sauce, the better . . . you can never have too much sauce. My point is that he's big on flavor and therefore has never been interested in white fish, like cod. He claims it's flavorless, but then he tasted this dish. His very words were "I could eat this every day." You see? Sometimes you can indeed prove your parents wrong. All it takes is a little squeeze of lemon, a touch of butter, a handful of fresh herbs, and a killer pan sauce to make a dish that's just as tasty as one full of lots of ingredients. If it happens to be citrus season when you make this, find yourself some Meyer lemons—their delicate flavor and sweetness are exceptionally delicious here.

2 tablespoons extra-virgin olive oil

4 (6- to 8-ounce) cod fillets

Kosher salt and freshly ground pepper

3 tablespoons all-purpose flour

2 tablespoons salted butter

1 Meyer or regular lemon, sliced, plus more for serving

1 garlic clove, minced or grated

1 bunch of asparagus, ends trimmed, cut into 1-inch pieces

1 cup uncooked orzo

2¾ cups low-sodium chicken broth

1 tablespoon lemon juice

1 tablespoon chopped fresh dill, for serving

1. In a large cast-iron skillet, heat the olive oil over medium-high heat. Season the cod all over with salt and pepper, then sprinkle it evenly on both sides with flour. When the oil shimmers, add the cod and sear until golden, 3 to 4 minutes per side. Transfer the cod to a plate.

2. Using the same skillet, sear the butter and lemon slices until the lemon is golden, about 1 minute per side. Add the lemon to the cod on the plate.

3. Again using the same skillet, cook the garlic, asparagus, and orzo until the garlic is fragrant and the orzo is toasted, 2 to 3 minutes. Add the chicken broth and lemon juice. Increase the heat to high and bring to a boil. Cook, stirring occasionally, until the orzo is al dente, about 10 minutes. Slide the cod, lemon slices, and any collected juices back into the skillet and cook until everything is warmed through, about 1 minute.

4. Top with fresh dill and serve.

SESAME-CRUSTED SALMON

WITH HONEY-SOY DRESSING

SERVES: 4

PREP TIME: 10 minutes
COOK TIME: 15 minutes
TOTAL TIME: 25 minutes

Sesame seeds make almost anything taste better. Especially when they're toasted and used in as prominent a way as they are here. I coat the salmon in a pretty mix of black and white sesame seeds and then pan-sear the fillets, keeping the skin on—doing so adds nice flavor and keeps the salmon from drying out. I know you might prefer skinless salmon, but I encourage you to try it my way. See if you like the results better— I think you just might. As the salmon cooks, the fat from the skin releases into the pan, and once the fillets are flipped, the sesame seeds slowly toast in the omega-3-rich fat. You don't want to waste all those healthy fats and delicious flavor, right?

¼ cup low-sodium soy sauce

3 tablespoons honey

1 (1-inch) piece of fresh ginger, peeled and grated

2 teaspoons orange zest

2 teaspoons chili sauce

¼ cup white sesame seeds

¼ cup black sesame seeds

4 (6- to 8-ounce) skin-on salmon fillets

1 egg white

3 tablespoons sesame oil

1. In a small bowl, whisk together the soy sauce, 2 tablespoons of the honey, the ginger, orange zest, and chili sauce.

2. In a separate small bowl, combine the white and black sesame seeds. Place the salmon on a large plate and brush the top of each fillet with egg white, then coat with the sesame seed mixture.

3. In a large skillet, heat the sesame oil over medium heat. When the oil shimmers, place the salmon in the skillet, sesame-seed side down. Cook until the sesame seeds are fragrant and toasted, 2 to 3 minutes. If the sesame seeds begin browning too quickly, reduce the heat to low. Carefully flip each fillet and cook until the salmon is crisp, 2 to 3 minutes more. During the last minute of cooking, drizzle the top of the salmon with the remaining 1 tablespoon of honey. Remove the pan from the heat.

4. Transfer the salmon to four plates and serve warm, with the soy dressing drizzled over the top.

MEDITERRANEAN
TUNA AND FOCACCIA SANDWICH

MAKES: 4 SANDWICHES

PREP TIME: 15 minutes
TOTAL TIME: 15 minutes

I debated just calling this recipe "pantry tuna lunch," but I ultimately decided that didn't sound quite as delicious. However, that's what this sandwich is, a mash-up of some of my favorite staples: sun-dried tomatoes, tuna, focaccia bread, and a good amount of herbs and arugula for freshness. It's quick to prepare, requires no cooking time, and is pretty healthy, too. Focaccia is the perfect bread to use since it holds up well and does not easily get soggy . . . it's also just really tasty. You can make it the night before, then grab and go in the morning for a quick and delicious lunch. It's also great for beachside picnics . . . or in my case, mountainside picnics.

1 (8-ounce) jar sun-dried tomatoes packed in olive oil, drained and oil reserved

Zest and juice of 2 lemons

½ cup fresh basil leaves, chopped

2 tablespoons chopped fresh dill

Kosher salt and freshly ground pepper

Pinch of crushed red pepper flakes

1 loaf focaccia bread, halved lengthwise

2 (5-ounce) cans oil-packed tuna

¼ cup pitted kalamata olives, chopped

1 roasted red pepper, chopped

2 cups fresh arugula

4 to 6 ounces feta cheese, crumbled

1. In a small bowl, whisk together the reserved olive oil, lemon zest, lemon juice, basil, and dill. Season with salt, pepper, and red pepper flakes. Using a spoon, drizzle and spread the oil on the cut sides of the focaccia.

2. Roughly chop the sun-dried tomatoes.

3. In a medium bowl, combine the tuna, olives, red pepper, and sun-dried tomatoes. Stir to mix well. Spread the tuna evenly over the bottom half of the focaccia. Top with arugula and sprinkle with feta. Add the top half of the focaccia and gently push down on the sandwich.

4. To serve, cut the focaccia into four equal pieces. Alternately, you can wrap the sandwich in plastic wrap and keep it in the fridge for up to 1 day.

. . . .

Ciabatta bread is a nice alternative to focaccia, as it also holds up well and does not get soggy.

10

ONE-POT SPANISH CHORIZO, SHRIMP, AND RICE PILAF

SERVES: 6

PREP TIME: 10 minutes
COOK TIME: 25 minutes
TOTAL TIME: 35 minutes

Why do I *love* one-pot recipes? Well, it's simple—for the same reason as you: I hate doing the dishes. Don't we all? After cooking dinner, the last thing I want to do is the dishes. This one-pot wonder is my quick version of jambalaya, and it's one of tastiest one-pot recipes you'll come across. The other thing I hate? Boring recipes—so, thankfully, this is not. The shrimp is seasoned with soulful and spicy Creole seasonings, plus you also have bell peppers, Spanish chorizo, and a spaghetti-rice mix. It might take you a bit longer than thirty minutes, but not too much longer—sometimes the extra time spent is well worth it.

3 tablespoons extra-virgin olive oil

1½ pounds large, raw, tail-on shrimp, peeled and deveined

1 tablespoon Homemade Creole Seasoning (page 58) or store-bought blend

1 teaspoon smoked paprika

1 teaspoon dried thyme

Kosher salt and freshly ground pepper

2 bell peppers, chopped

½ pound Spanish chorizo (casing removed), cubed

⅓ cup uncooked, broken spaghetti (see Notes)

1 cup uncooked basmati rice

Juice of 1 lemon (see Notes)

¼ cup fresh parsley, chopped

1. In a medium bowl, combine 2 tablespoons of the olive oil, the shrimp, Creole seasoning, paprika, thyme, and a pinch each of salt and pepper. Toss to coat.

2. Heat a large skillet over medium-high heat. Add the shrimp in a single layer and cook until seared, 2 to 3 minutes. Add the bell peppers and chorizo and cook, stirring occasionally, until the shrimp is pink and cooked through, 3 to 5 minutes more. Transfer the shrimp mixture to a large plate.

3. In the same skillet, heat the remaining 1 tablespoon of olive oil over medium heat. When the oil shimmers, add the spaghetti and rice and cook until toasted, 1 to 2 minutes. Stir in 2 cups of water, increase the heat to high, and bring to a boil. Cover, reduce the heat to low, and cook for 5 minutes. Turn the heat off and let the rice and spaghetti sit, covered, until it's fluffy, about 15 minutes more (no peeking).

4. Remove the lid and fluff the rice with a fork. Return the shrimp and peppers to the skillet and toss to combine.

5. Divide the jambalaya among six plates and finish with lemon juice and parsley.

. . . .

To make broken spaghetti, just take a handful of dry spaghetti and break it up into 3 or 4 pieces. Now you have broken spaghetti!

. . . .

I use the juice of one whole lemon for this, but I love lemon. If you're worried it might be too much for you, start with half and add more to taste.

DESSERT

STRAWBERRY NAKED CAKE

. . . .
SERVES: 16
. . . .

PREP TIME: 1 hour
COOK TIME: 30 minutes
TOTAL TIME: 1 hour 30 minutes,
plus cooling time

I love a layer cake. It's no secret. They're my specialty, but maybe not for the reasons you may think. As much as I love baking them, I love decorating and styling out cakes just as much. I grew up putting together outfits while sitting on the floor of my grandma's closet, arranging dinner tables like it was my job, and decorating for the holidays like a ten-year-old Martha Stewart. I've always loved to make everything I touch look the prettiest it can—and this *especially* applies to cakes. I do them up with chocolate curls, berries, flowers, whatever fits the recipe. Here's the thing, though: layer cakes can be time consuming, requiring multiple pans and hours of prep work and cooling. My trick? Doing it on a baking sheet! It's genius and easy and you are going to love it.

Butter, for greasing

1 cup canola oil

¾ cup full-fat plain Greek yogurt

4 large eggs, at room temperature

2 cups granulated sugar

1 tablespoon pure vanilla extract

1¾ cups buttermilk,
at room temperature

4 cups all-purpose flour

1½ teaspoons baking soda

1½ teaspoons baking powder

1½ teaspoons kosher salt

Zest of 1 lemon

¾ cup high-quality strawberry jam

3 cups fresh strawberries, sliced

WHITE CHOCOLATE BUTTERCREAM

2 cups (4 sticks) salted butter,
at room temperature

2 cups confectioners' sugar

8 ounces white chocolate,
melted and cooled

1. Preheat the oven to 350°F. Grease a 13 × 18-inch rimmed baking sheet and line it with parchment paper, leaving a 1-inch overhang on the two long sides. Lightly grease the parchment paper.

2. **Make the cake.** In a stand mixer fitted with the paddle attachment, beat together the canola oil, yogurt, eggs, granulated sugar, vanilla, and buttermilk until smooth. With the mixer on low, slowly add the flour, baking soda, baking powder, salt, and lemon zest and mix until just combined, about 2 minutes.

3. Pour the batter onto the prepared baking sheet. Bake until the top is just set and no longer wiggly in the center, 25 to 30 minutes. Remove the cake from the oven and run a knife around the outside edge to loosen it from the paper. Let it cool completely in the pan, about 1 hour.

4. **Meanwhile, make the buttercream.** In a stand mixer fitted with the paddle attachment, beat together the butter and confectioners' sugar until light and fluffy, 3 to 5 minutes. Add the melted white chocolate and beat until combined, about 1 minute.

5. **Assemble the cake.** Using the parchment paper overhang, carefully lift the cake from the baking sheet. With a sharp serrated knife, cut the cake evenly into 3 rectangular pieces (about 13 × 6 inches each)—these will be your layers. Then, using scissors, carefully cut through the parchment paper, leaving the paper intact underneath each layer of cake to help you stack the layers. Evenly trim the edges of the cake.

6. Place one cake layer on a serving plate with the parchment face down. Using a knife or an offset spatula, spread one-third of the buttercream all the way to the edge. Add half the jam, lightly swirling it into the buttercream. Top with 1 cup of the sliced strawberries, being careful not to overfill the layers. Repeat with the second cake layer. Add the third cake layer and lightly frost the top of the cake with the remaining buttercream. Decorate the top with the remaining 1 cup of strawberries before serving. Store any leftovers refrigerated in an airtight container for up to 1 day.

Let the parchment help you place the second and third layers of cake. Use it as a "handle" to lift and invert the cake layer onto the frosting of the first layer. Once the second layer is in place, peel off the parchment and frost the cake. Repeat with the third and final layer.

BLACKOUT CHOCOLATE CAKE

SERVES: 16

PREP TIME: 1 hour
COOK TIME: 30 minutes
TOTAL TIME: 1 hour 30 minutes,
plus cooling time

Three layers of dark, mysterious, chocolatey goodness. This cake is nothing short of delicious—and an absolute dream. Every bite is richer than the last. What could be better than chocolate on chocolate . . . times three?

BLACKOUT CHOCOLATE CAKE

Butter, for greasing

4 eggs, at room temperature (see Note)

1¾ cups buttermilk, at room temperature

1 cup canola oil

1 tablespoon pure vanilla extract

2 cups all-purpose flour

2 cups unsweetened cocoa powder

2 cups granulated sugar

3 teaspoons baking soda

3 teaspoons baking powder

2 teaspoons kosher salt

¾ cup hot black coffee

WHIPPED CHOCOLATE BUTTERCREAM

2 cups (4 sticks) salted butter, at room temperature

4 cups confectioners' sugar

1 cup unsweetened cocoa powder

1 tablespoon vanilla extract

3 tablespoons heavy whipping cream

1. Preheat the oven to 350°F. Grease a 13 × 18-inch rimmed baking sheet and line it with parchment paper, leaving a 1-inch overhang on the two long sides. Lightly grease the parchment paper.

2. **Make the cake.** In a stand mixer fitted with the paddle attachment, beat together the eggs, buttermilk, canola oil, and vanilla until smooth. With the mixer on low, slowly add the flour, cocoa powder, granulated sugar, baking soda, baking powder, and salt and mix just until no clumps of flour remain, about 2 minutes. Add the coffee and mix until just combined, about 1 minute more. The batter should be pourable, but not super thin.

3. Pour the batter onto the prepared baking sheet. Bake until the top is just set and no longer wiggly in the center, 25 to 30 minutes. Remove the cake from the oven and run a knife around the outside edge to loosen it from the paper. Let it cool completely in the pan, about 1 hour.

4. **Meanwhile, make the buttercream.** In a stand mixer fitted with the paddle attachment, beat together the butter and confectioners' sugar until light and fluffy, 3 to 5 minutes. Add the cocoa powder and vanilla and beat, scraping down the sides as needed, until no streaks of white remain, about 2 minutes more. Add the heavy cream and whip until light and fluffy, about 1 minute more.

5. **Assemble the cake.** Using the parchment paper overhang, carefully lift the cake from the baking sheet. With a sharp serrated knife, cut the cake evenly into 3 rectangular pieces (about 13 × 6 inches each)—these will be your layers. Then, using scissors, carefully cut through the parchment paper, leaving the paper intact underneath each layer of cake to help you stack the layers. Evenly trim the edges of the layers of the cake.

6. Place one cake layer on a serving plate. Using a knife or an offset spatula, spread one-third of the buttercream all the way to the edge. Place the second layer on top and spread another third of the buttercream all the way to the edge. Add the third layer and spread the remaining buttercream evenly over the top and down the sides of the cake. Crumble the reserved cake trimmings and press them into the sides of the cake to coat.

7. Store the cake at room temperature loosely covered for up to 2 days.

To quickly bring eggs to room temperature, place them in a bowl and fill it with warm water. Let them sit 5 minutes.

COCONUT CARROT CAKE

SERVES: 16

PREP TIME: 1 hour
COOK TIME: 30 minutes
TOTAL TIME: 1 hour 30 minutes,
plus cooling time

The idea of carrot cake has always sounded a bit off to me. Don't get me wrong, I love carrots, but I love them roasted or raw—why would I want them in my cake? It's always something I wondered about, but then I experienced my first slice of homemade carrot cake and my views on carrot cake changed forever. I finally understood what all the hype was about. Not only do the carrots add moistness to the cake, the sweet flavor they give off is surprisingly delicious. I kept the flavors and elements of a traditional carrot cake but added sweet coconut for a tropical touch, swirled dried berries into the cream cheese frosting for a pop of pretty pink color, and decorated with fresh flowers . . . some people decorate with sprinkles, but then there's me, and flowers are the sprinkles in my life.

Butter, for greasing
1½ cups canola oil
¾ cup buttermilk
3 eggs, at room temperature
1 cup granulated sugar
½ cup packed light brown sugar
2 teaspoons pure vanilla extract

1 pound carrots, grated
1 cup sweetened shredded coconut
3 cups all-purpose flour
1½ teaspoons baking powder
1½ teaspoons baking soda
1 teaspoon ground cinnamon
1 teaspoon kosher salt

CREAM CHEESE FROSTING

8 ounces cream cheese, at room temperature
1 cup (2 sticks) salted butter, at room temperature
2 to 3 cups confectioners' sugar

2 teaspoons pure vanilla extract
1 cup freeze-dried strawberries or raspberries, ground to a fine powder (optional)

1. Preheat the oven to 350°F. Grease a 13 × 18-inch rimmed baking sheet and line it with parchment paper, leaving a 1-inch overhang on the two long sides. Lightly grease the parchment paper.

2. **Make the cake.** In a stand mixer fitted with the paddle attachment, beat together the canola oil, buttermilk, eggs, granulated sugar, brown sugar, and vanilla until smooth. Beat in the carrots and coconut. With the mixer on low, slowly add the flour, baking powder, baking soda, cinnamon, and salt. Mix just until there are no longer any clumps of flour, about 2 minutes.

3. Pour the batter onto the prepared baking sheet. Bake until the top is just set and no longer wiggly in the center, 25 to 30 minutes. Remove the cake from the oven and run a knife around the outside edge to loosen it from the paper. Let it cool completely in the pan, about 1 hour.

4. **Meanwhile, make the frosting.** In a stand mixer fitted with the paddle attachment, beat together the cream cheese and butter until light and fluffy, about 2 minutes. Add the confectioners' sugar and vanilla, beating until combined, about 2 minutes more. Beat in the berry powder (if using).

5. **Assemble the cake.** Using the parchment paper overhang, carefully lift the cake from the baking sheet. With a sharp serrated knife, cut the cake evenly into 3 rectangular layers (about 13 × 6 inches each)—these will be your layers. Then, using scissors, carefully cut through the parchment paper, leaving the paper intact underneath each layer of cake to help you stack the layers.

6. Place one cake layer on a serving plate. With a knife or an offset spatula, spread one-third of the frosting all the way to the edge. Place the second layer on top and spread another third of the buttercream all the way to the edge. Add the third layer and spread the remaining frosting over the top. Serve or store refrigerated in an airtight container for up to 1 day.

EASIEST CINNAMON-APPLE TARTS

. . . .

MAKES: 6 TARTS

. . . .

PREP TIME: 15 minutes
COOK TIME: 30 minutes
TOTAL TIME: 45 minutes

I might be judged for saying this, but I can live with that. . . .

Why would you spend time making pastry dough when there's a perfect version available at the supermarket? It's truthfully so good, I keep it stocked in my freezer at all times. Here, I use it to make these cute little apple tarts, which are a true favorite among everyone who's had them. I recommend using smaller apples—that way half an apple will fit into each tart, allowing you to create a fanned look. It won't make a difference in the taste, but it sure is pretty (and we all know pretty food might actually taste just a little bit better). I love these warm, right out of the oven. And while it's definitely not necessary, a scoop of vanilla ice cream is a great idea with these tarts.

⅓ cup packed light brown sugar

2 tablespoons salted butter, at room temperature

1 tablespoon brandy or bourbon

1 teaspoon pure vanilla extract

1 teaspoon ground cinnamon

1 sheet frozen puff pastry, thawed (see Note)

2 large or 3 small Honeycrisp apples, cored, halved, and thinly sliced

2 tablespoons melted butter, for brushing

Vanilla ice cream, for serving

1. Preheat the oven to 400°F. Line a rimmed baking sheet with parchment paper.

2. In a small bowl, stir together the sugar, butter, brandy, vanilla, and cinnamon.

3. Cut the puff pastry sheet into 6 equal rectangles and transfer them to the prepared baking sheet. Spread about 2 teaspoons of the sugar mixture onto each square.

4. Arrange the apple slices, skin side up, on each piece of pastry. Fold the edges of the pastry inward, pressing to seal the corners. Evenly drizzle the remaining sugar mixture on the apples. Brush the edges of pastry with the melted butter.

5. Bake until the pastry is golden and the apples are tender, 25 to 30 minutes. Serve the tarts warm, topped with vanilla ice cream. Store any leftovers at room temperature in an airtight container for up to 3 days.

. . . .

If you forget to thaw your pastry in the fridge, you can place the pastry in the microwave to thaw (leave it in the paper bag, but take it out of the box). Simply heat it in 1-minute intervals on power level 1, flipping the pastry over after each minute, until it is almost thawed. Thawing time will vary depending on the strength of your microwave, but it usually takes me 2 to 3 minutes to thaw one sheet.

BOURBON-PEACH PANDOWDY

SERVES: 8

PREP TIME: 20 minutes
COOK TIME: 50 minutes
TOTAL TIME: 1 hour 10 minutes

Nothing screams summertime to me more than fresh peaches. This pandowdy is a deliciously sweet way to use up all those juicy beauties you may have sitting on your counter come late August. What's a pandowdy? It's similar to a peach pie, but baked in a skillet with cut-up pieces of dough on top. Cutting the pastry into large pieces, instead of leaving it whole, allows the caramel-like sauce to slowly bubble up and over and out. The last step is to spoon heavy cream over the top of the pandowdy, just before it's done baking, creating an almost custard-like filling. It. Is. Soooo. Gooood!

6 tablespoons salted butter

4 to 5 cups sliced fresh peaches (see Note)

3 tablespoons dark brown sugar

1 tablespoon all-purpose flour

2 tablespoons bourbon

2 teaspoons pure vanilla extract

Juice of ½ lemon

1 teaspoon ground cinnamon

½ teaspoon ground ginger

½ teaspoon kosher salt (see Note)

1 sheet frozen puff pastry, thawed

1 large egg, beaten

Coarse sugar, for topping

⅓ cup heavy cream

Vanilla ice cream, for serving (optional)

1. Preheat the oven to 425°F.

2. In a 10-inch oven-safe skillet, melt the butter over medium heat and cook until lightly browned, 3 to 5 minutes. Remove the skillet from the heat.

3. In a large bowl, combine the peaches, brown sugar, flour, bourbon, vanilla, lemon juice, cinnamon, ginger, and salt. Toss to coat. Add the mixture to the butter in the skillet and gently mix to coat.

4. Place the sheet of pastry over the peaches and press down gently, tucking the sides of the pastry under the peaches as best you can. Brush the pastry with the beaten egg and sprinkle with coarse sugar. Place the skillet on a baking sheet and bake until the top of the pastry is lightly browned, about 20 minutes.

5. Remove the skillet from the oven and, using a sharp knife, cut the pastry into large squares, creating a crosshatch pattern. Reduce the oven temperature to 350°F and return the skillet to the oven. Bake until the liquid is bubbling up through the cracks in the pastry, about 20 minutes more. If the pastry begins to burn, cover the skillet with aluminum foil.

6. Remove the skillet from the oven, spoon the heavy cream over the pastry, and return the skillet to the oven once more. Bake until the pastry is dark golden brown, about 10 minutes more.

7. Using a spoon, press the pastry down into the juices, but don't quite submerge it. Serve the pandowdy warm from the skillet, with ice cream alongside, if desired. Store any leftovers refrigerated in an airtight container for up to 3 days.

You can use frozen peaches, but do not thaw them first. Instead, add about 5 minutes to the cooking time. When peaches are out of season, you can use apples instead.

STRAWBERRY PRETZEL TART

WITH WHIPPED MASCARPONE

SERVES: 8

PREP TIME: 20 minutes
COOK TIME: 10 minutes
TOTAL TIME: 30 minutes

This is my version of strawberry pretzel salad, a dessert that originated in the South. Why was/is it called "pretzel salad"? That's what everyone wants to know . . . and debates. It's said to be called a "salad" because in the 1950s, '60s, and '70s, anything that was made with Jell-O was called a "salad." Honestly, it makes zero sense to me, but this is my updated take on the recipe, minus the retro ingredients and plus whipped mascarpone. It's simply made, using crushed pretzels for the crust and honey to sweeten things up. The thick layer of mascarpone cheese is the perfect delicate flavor to pair with the sweet strawberries and a touch of lemon juice. If available, finish the tart off with chamomile flowers for the prettiest spring and summer dessert or a beautiful brunch dish.

2 cups finely crushed salted pretzels

1 large egg, beaten

6 tablespoons salted butter, melted

4 tablespoons honey, plus more for serving

4 ounces mascarpone or cream cheese

1 tablespoon lemon juice

⅓ cup heavy cream

1 to 2 teaspoons lemon zest

2 cups sliced fresh strawberries

Chamomile flowers, for garnish (optional)

1. Preheat the oven to 350°F. Line a rimmed baking sheet with parchment paper.

2. **Make the crust.** In a medium bowl, stir together the pretzel crumbs, egg, butter, and 3 tablespoons of the honey until well combined. Pat the mixture onto the prepared baking sheet, pressing firmly into the bottom of the sheet until about ¼ inch thick. Bake until toasted, 10 to 15 minutes. Let cool completely, 10 to 15 minutes.

3. **Make the whipped mascarpone.** Meanwhile, in a medium bowl, using an electric mixer, whip together the mascarpone and lemon juice until smooth, about 1 minute. Slowly add the cream and whip until soft peaks form, 2 to 3 minutes. Add the remaining 1 tablespoon of honey and the lemon zest and whip until combined, about 1 minute more. Spread the mixture over the cooled crust.

4. Just before serving, arrange the strawberries over the mascarpone. Drizzle the tart with honey and garnish with the flowers, if desired.

To make this dessert ahead of time, you can bake the crust and whip the mascarpone a day or two before, but keep them separate until you're ready to serve. The mascarpone will keep in the fridge for up to 2 days, and the crust can be kept at room temperature wrapped in plastic wrap for 3 days. Once assembled, the tart can be stored refrigerated for 1 day; beyond that, the pretzels will begin to get soggy.

SLICE & BAKE

SNICKER-DOODLES

WITH EGGNOG FROSTING

MAKES: ABOUT 4 DOZEN COOKIES

PREP TIME: 40 minutes
COOK TIME: 10 minutes
TOTAL TIME: 50 minutes, plus chilling

These are some of the best holiday cookies ever. I'm being serious. Sugar cookie dough, rolled in cinnamon sugar, and a light and fluffy eggnog frosting. Yes, they're *delicious*—and a million times easier than hand-rolling dozens of cookie-dough balls in cinnamon sugar. And this recipe is for sure the best use of the holiday eggnog that's been sitting in your fridge. If you don't have an entire day to spend baking holiday cookies (or really, even if you do), make these. Everyone coming over for Christmas will be so happy you did! You can store unfrosted cookies in an airtight container at room temperature for up to 4 days. Frosted cookies will keep in an airtight container in the refrigerator for up to 1 week.

They're also are a great addition to holiday boxes. Bake as directed, but leave the cookies unfrosted. Instead, package up the frosting in a cute jar to gift along with the cookies.

SNICKERDOODLE COOKIES

1½ cups (3 sticks) salted butter, at room temperature

1¼ cups granulated sugar

1 tablespoon pure vanilla extract

2 large eggs

4½ cups all-purpose flour

1 teaspoon baking soda

¾ teaspoon ground cinnamon

CINNAMON SUGAR COATING

½ cup granulated sugar

1 tablespoon ground cinnamon

EGGNOG FROSTING

½ cup (1 stick) salted butter, at room temperature

2 cups confectioners' sugar

2 to 4 tablespoons high-quality eggnog (see Note)

1. **Make the cookie dough.** In a stand mixer fitted with the paddle attachment, cream together the butter, sugar, and vanilla on medium speed until light and fluffy, 3 to 5 minutes. Add the eggs and beat until evenly combined. Add the flour, baking soda, and the ¾ teaspoon of cinnamon and beat until combined and a dough forms.

2. Divide the dough into 2 balls and place each on a large piece of wax paper. Using your hands, shape each ball of dough into a 10-inch log.

3. **Make the cinnamon sugar.** In a small bowl, combine the granulated sugar and the 1 tablespoon of cinnamon. Working on the wax paper, generously coat each log in cinnamon sugar. Reserve any excess. Wrap each log tightly in the wax paper and chill in the fridge for at least 1 hour or up to 3 days.

4. Preheat the oven to 350°F. Line a rimmed baking sheet with parchment paper or a silicone mat.

5. Unwrap the dough and slice each log crosswise into 20 to 24 equal rounds. Place the rounds on the prepared baking sheet, spacing them ½ inch apart. Bake until the cookies are set on the edges, 8 to 10 minutes.

6. Let the cookies cool on the baking sheet for 5 minutes, then transfer them to a wire rack to cool completely.

7. **Meanwhile, make the frosting.** In a stand mixer fitted with the paddle attachment, beat together the butter and confectioners' sugar until creamy. Slowly add the eggnog and beat to combine.

8. Using an offset spatula, frost each cookie and sprinkle any remaining cinnamon sugar on top.

The cookie dough can also be stored in the freezer wrapped tightly in plastic wrap and placed in a zip-top bag or an airtight plastic container for up to 3 months. When you're ready to use it, remove the dough from the freezer and let it thaw for 5 minutes before slicing, then bake as directed.

If you don't have eggnog on hand, use equal amounts of heavy cream plus 1 tablespoon pure vanilla extract or bourbon.

BUTTER PECAN BARS

WITH CHOCOLATE AND COCONUT

MAKES: 9 BARS

PREP TIME: 25 minutes
COOK TIME: 35 minutes
TOTAL TIME: 1 hour, plus cooling time

Addicting. That's the best way I can think of to describe this recipe. Let me explain: Think shortbread cookie dough layered with chocolate chips and a gooey coconut pecan sauce that tastes almost like butterscotch. All of it gets baked together until the chocolate has melted and the sauce has thickened and caramelized on top. The caramelization creates a bit of a crunchy topping, making every single bite *so* good. These bars are decadent, but so easy, and are perfect for serving family and friends. They are equally perfect for giving in to a serious coconut-chocolate fix.

12 tablespoons (1½ sticks) salted butter, at room temperature

1¼ cups packed light brown sugar

3 teaspoons pure vanilla extract

1¼ cups all-purpose flour

⅔ cup heavy cream

1½ cups roughly chopped pecans

1½ cups shredded unsweetened coconut (see Note)

2 cups semisweet chocolate chips

1. Preheat the oven to 350°F. Line an 8 × 8-inch baking dish with parchment paper or grease a 9-inch round pie plate with butter or cooking spray.

2. **Make the dough.** In a stand mixer fitted with the paddle attachment, beat 8 tablespoons of the butter, ¼ cup of the sugar, and 1 teaspoon of the vanilla together until smooth, about 1 minute. Add the flour and 1 teaspoon of water and beat to combine well, 2 minutes more.

3. Press the dough into the bottom and up the sides of the prepared baking dish. Bake until the crust is lightly golden, about 10 minutes. Remove the pan from the oven, but leave the oven on.

4. **Meanwhile, make the sauce.** In a medium saucepan, place the remaining 4 tablespoons of butter, the cream, the remaining 1 cup of sugar, and the remaining 2 teaspoons of vanilla. Bring to a boil over medium heat and cook, stirring often, until the sugar has dissolved and the sauce has thickened slightly, about 5 minutes. Remove the saucepan from the heat and stir in the pecans and coconut.

5. Scatter the chocolate chips evenly over the crust. Pour the pecan and coconut mixture over the chocolate and, using a spatula, gently spread to distribute it evenly. Bake until the top begins to brown and caramelize, 20 to 25 minutes.

6. Allow the bars to cool for about 20 minutes, then slice and serve warm or at room temperature. Store in an airtight container at room temperature for 3 to 4 days.

. . . .

I like using unsweetened coconut, but if you prefer a sweeter bar, use the sweetened variety.

CHOCOLATE MOUSSE

SERVES: 4 TO 6

PREP TIME: 10 minutes
TOTAL TIME: 10 minutes, plus chilling

If you've ever made a traditional chocolate mousse, you know that the process is a bit tedious and can often end in a soupy mess . . . or I don't know, maybe that's just me? Regardless, I've never been able to master a perfect chocolate mousse. That is, of course, until I whipped up this ten-minute mousse that's the chocolate dessert of my dreams. It's egg-free, light, airy, chocolaty, perfectly sweet, and beyond good. If you can make whipped cream, you can make this chocolate mousse. It's the easiest mousse recipe ever, requiring only six ingredients and one bowl. Enjoy it by the spoonful.

CHOCOLATE MOUSSE

4 ounces cream cheese, at room temperature

1 cup heavy cream

½ cup whole milk

⅓ cup unsweetened cocoa powder

¼ cup confectioners' sugar, plus more as needed

2 teaspoons pure vanilla extract

WHIPPED CRÈME FRAÎCHE

4 ounces crème fraîche

2 teaspoons confectioners' sugar

Milk- or dark-chocolate shavings, for garnish

1. **Make the mousse.** In a stand mixer fitted with the whisk attachment, combine the cream cheese and heavy cream on high speed until soft peaks form, 3 to 5 minutes. On medium speed, slowly add the milk, cocoa powder, ¼ cup of confectioners' sugar, and the vanilla and whisk (being careful to not overmix) until smooth, 1 to 2 minutes. Taste and add more confectioners' sugar as needed.

2. Divide the mousse among four to six small bowls. Cover with plastic wrap and chill for at least 1 hour or up to 3 days.

3. **Meanwhile, make the whipped crème fraîche.** In a stand mixer fitted with the whisk attachment, combine the crème fraîche and the 2 teaspoons of confectioners' sugar and whip until light and fluffy, about 1 minute.

4. Top the mousse with whipped crème fraîche and garnish with chocolate shavings.

SWIRLED BANANA BUNDT CAKE

SERVES: 8

PREP TIME: 15 minutes
COOK TIME: 45 minutes
TOTAL TIME: 1 hour

I don't like to play favorites, but if I *had* to choose a favorite dessert, I think it just might be this cake. In fact, the cake itself is so delicious that I didn't even add a frosting or a glaze—and I've never *not* added frosting or glaze to a cake until this one, which should tell you something major. What makes this so good? (1) Extra-ripe bananas (think blackened): They keep the cake moist while also sweetening it. (2) A dash of cinnamon: It adds a touch of warmth, which is rather nice when paired with the sweet bananas. (3) Cream cheese: It might seem odd in a banana cake, but trust me on this one—it makes for tender perfection. Since this cake is made with both bananas and cream cheese, I'm pretty sure it is an acceptable breakfast item. Yes, chocolate chips and all.

12 tablespoons (1½ sticks) salted butter, at room temperature, plus more for greasing

¾ cup packed light brown sugar

2 teaspoons pure vanilla extract

3 large eggs

2 cups mashed banana

2½ cups all-purpose flour

2 teaspoons baking powder

½ teaspoon baking soda

1½ teaspoons ground cinnamon

½ teaspoon kosher salt

2 cups chopped semisweet chocolate

8 ounces cream cheese, at room temperature

1. Preheat the oven to 400°F. Grease a 10-inch Bundt pan with butter.

2. In a stand mixer fitted with the paddle attachment, combine the butter, sugar, and vanilla and beat on medium speed until fluffy, about 5 minutes. Add the eggs one at a time and beat until fully incorporated. Add the mashed banana and beat until combined, about 1 minute. Add the flour, baking powder, baking soda, cinnamon, and salt and mix on low speed until just combined, 1 to 2 minutes. Using a spatula, fold in the chocolate chips.

3. Place the cream cheese in a small, microwave-safe bowl and microwave on high until almost melted, 30 to 45 seconds.

4. Spoon half of the banana batter into the prepared pan. Gently spoon the softened cream cheese on top of the batter and, using a spatula, spread it in an even layer, swirling it gently. Layer the remaining banana batter on top. Bake until a toothpick inserted into the center of the cake comes out clean, 40 to 45 minutes.

5. Let the cake cool for 15 minutes, then invert it onto a plate. Slice and serve slightly warm or at room temperature. Store any leftovers refrigerated in plastic wrap for up to 3 days.

CHOCOLATE PEANUT BUTTER

BLONDIE BROWNIE BARS

MAKES: 14 BARS

PREP TIME: 15 minutes
COOK TIME: 25 minutes
TOTAL TIME: 40 minutes,
plus cooling time

You might think you love the combination of chocolate and peanut butter, but I think I might love it more than anyone. These bars are decadent and nutty, chocolaty and fudgy, and *sooooo* above yummy. Bring them to school potlucks and, without fail, you will be the most popular parent in the room . . . or in my case, big sister in the room, because the only kid on my radar right now is my favorite little sister, Asher. She begs me to make these every other week. They are her favorite. She's claimed them to be better than a peanut butter cup. If you knew Asher, you'd know this is saying a lot.

6 tablespoons salted butter, melted, plus more for greasing

1 (13.9-ounce) box brownie mix (see Note)

4 large eggs

10 tablespoons salted butter, at room temperature

¾ cup creamy peanut butter

1 cup packed light brown sugar

1 tablespoon pure vanilla extract

2 cups all-purpose flour

1 teaspoon baking powder

2 to 3 ounces milk- or dark-chocolate chunks

Flaky sea salt, for serving

1. Preheat the oven to 350°F. Grease a 9 × 13-inch baking dish.

2. **Make the brownies.** In a medium bowl, whisk together the brownie mix, melted butter, 2 eggs, and 1 tablespoon of water. Transfer the batter to the prepared baking dish.

3. **Make the blondies.** In a medium microwave-safe mixing bowl, combine the 10 tablespoons of butter and ½ cup of the peanut butter and microwave on high until melted, stirring every 30 seconds. Stir in the sugar, remaining 2 eggs, and vanilla. Add the flour and baking powder and stir to combine.

4. Layer half of the peanut butter dough on top of the brownie batter in the pan. Microwave the remaining ¼ cup of peanut butter on high until melted. Gently swirl the melted peanut butter into the dough in the pan. Layer the remaining dough on top (don't worry if it doesn't completely cover the melted peanut butter).

5. Bake until the center is just set, 20 to 22 minutes. Remove the baking dish from the oven and sprinkle the milk chocolate over the blondies. Return the baking dish to the oven and bake until the chocolate has melted, 1 to 2 minutes more.

6. Sprinkle the blondies with flaky salt and let cool completely in the pan before cutting, at least 1 hour. Cut into bars to serve. Store at room temperature in an airtight container for up to 5 days.

When it comes to brownie mixes, I'm very particular. I like Foodstirs Organic Chocolate Lovers Brownie Mix. You can find it in the baking aisle of most grocery stores or order it online.

CHEWY BROWNED-BUTTER
CHOCOLATE CHIP COOKIES

....

MAKES: 20 COOKIES

....

PREP TIME: 30 minutes
COOK TIME: 10 minutes
TOTAL TIME: 40 minutes,
plus cooling time

I wasn't sure the classic chocolate chip cookie could really be improved upon, but like most things in life, there's always room for a little improvement . . . and browned butter. The true secret to cookie baking success. These are the cookies to make when you need to impress friends, your new significant other, or the in-laws. Or do as I do . . . simply bake these up when you're in need of a warm cookie to sink your teeth into at the end of a very long day. I know food shouldn't be used as a stress reliever, but sorry, I don't understand that. Cookies always make things better.

1 cup (2 sticks) salted butter

¾ cup packed light brown sugar

¼ cup granulated sugar

2 large eggs

1 tablespoon pure vanilla extract

2¼ cups all-purpose flour

1 teaspoon baking soda

¼ teaspoon kosher salt

1½ cups semisweet chocolate chips

½ cup semisweet or dark chocolate chunks

Flaky sea salt, for serving (optional)

1. Preheat the oven to 350°F. Line a rimmed baking sheet with parchment paper.

2. **Make the browned butter.** In a medium skillet, melt ½ cup of the butter over medium heat. Cook, stirring often, until browned, 2 to 3 minutes. Remove the skillet from the heat and let the browned butter cool slightly. Transfer to a heatproof bowl and stick in the freezer to cool off completely, 10 to 15 minutes.

3. **Make the dough.** In a stand mixer fitted with the paddle attachment, beat the browned butter, the remaining ½ cup of butter, the brown sugar, and the granulated sugar until combined, 2 to 3 minutes. Add the eggs and vanilla and beat until creamy, about 1 minute. Add the flour, baking soda, and salt and beat until combined, about 1 minute. Fold in the chocolate chips and chocolate chunks.

4. Using your hands, roll the dough into rounded tablespoon-size balls. Place on the prepared baking sheet, spacing the cookies about 2 inches apart.

5. Bake until the cookies are just beginning to set on the edges but are still doughy in the center, 8 to 10 minutes. Let the cookies cool for 5 minutes on the baking sheet. Sprinkle with flaky salt, if desired, and eat them warm (highly recommended) or let them cool and store at room temperature in an airtight container for up to 4 days.

. . . .

If your kitchen gets warm and your dough is feeling sticky, pop the bowl of dough into the freezer for 10 to 15 minutes before you roll it into balls.

FUDGY ICE CREAM PRETZEL CAKE

SERVES: 8 TO 10

PREP TIME: 30 minutes
COOK TIME: 5 minutes
TOTAL TIME: 35 minutes
CHILL TIME: 8 hours

This cake is for you if you love dessert, but don't love baking. If you can mix together a few ingredients on the stove and make some layers out of store-bought ingredients, then you can handle this cake. Hold on—if you can't wrap your head around the idea of making fudge sauce, on the stove, well, that's no problem either—you can pick up your favorite chocolate sauce while you're at the store. I will not lie, homemade is better in this instance, but do what you have to do to get this cake made because it is not a cake you want to miss out on.

1 (14 ounce) can sweetened condensed milk

2 (3.5 ounce) bars high-quality semisweet or dark chocolate, chopped

3 teaspoons pure vanilla extract

6 tablespoons salted butter

2 quarts vanilla ice cream (4 pints), softened

3 cups mini pretzel twists

1½ cups heavy cream

1 to 3 tablespoons confectioners' sugar, to your taste

1. Line an 8-inch-square cake pan with parchment paper, leaving a 6-inch overhang on two sides. Or use and 8-inch springform pan. Chill in the freezer for at least 15 minutes.

2. Meanwhile, make the fudge sauce. In a medium saucepan, combine the sweetened condensed milk, chocolate, 2 teaspoons of the vanilla, and 3 tablespoons of the butter. Cook over medium heat, stirring constantly, 5 minutes or until the butter and chocolate are melted and the sauce is smooth. Remove from the heat. Let cool, 10 to 15 minutes.

3. Press 2 pints of the softened ice cream into the chilled pan. Swirl in half of the fudge sauce, then top with an even layer of pretzels, about 1 cup. Freeze for 1 hour. Repeat with the remaining 2 pints of ice cream, remaining fudge sauce (re-warm if needed to loosen it), and end with a layer of pretzels, about 1 cup. Cover the cake with plastic wrap and freeze until completely firm, at least 8 hours or overnight.

4. Lift the cake out of the pan using the parchment paper overhang and place it on a serving plate. Freeze for another 30 minutes to reset or until ready to serve.

5. Meanwhile, crush the remaining 1 cup of pretzels into crumbs. In a skillet, melt the remaining 3 tablespoons butter over medium heat. Allow the butter to brown until it smells toasted and is a deep golden brown, 3 to 4 minutes. Stir in the pretzels and cook another minute, until toasted. Remove from the heat and transfer the crumbs to a plate. Let cool.

6. Just before serving, whip the cream. In a medium bowl, using handheld mixer, whip the cream until soft peaks form. Add the powdered sugar and remaining 1 teaspoon vanilla and whip until combined.

7. Top the cake with the whipped cream and sprinkle it with the toasted pretzel crumbs. Serve immediately.

. . . . . .

Remove the ice cream 10 minutes before using to allow it to soften slightly. I find it easiest to buy three separate 1-pint containers of ice cream. This method makes softening the ice cream easier, so that by the end of the assembly you won't wind up with a soupy mess.

BLACKBERRY LAVENDER BUCKLE

....

SERVES: 6 TO 8

....

PREP TIME: 15 minutes
COOK TIME: 55 minutes
TOTAL TIME: 1 hour 10 minutes,
plus cooling time

What is a buckle, you ask? Simply put, it's just a word for a fruit-filled cake topped with a buttery streusel. The streusel topping makes the cake look "buckled," hence the name. Well, every bite of this buckle is layered with fresh berries, hints of lavender, and sweet vanilla. You can eat it right out of the oven, no cooling required. It's great for dessert or even for brunch. Oh, and you'll earn major bonus points if you top it with ice cream. Definitely not needed, but highly recommended.

½ cup (1 stick) salted butter, melted, plus more for greasing

1½ cups Everyday Pancake Mix (page 17; see Notes)

2 teaspoons dried culinary lavender (see Notes)

1 cup packed light brown sugar

⅔ cup whole milk

2 large eggs

2 teaspoons pure vanilla extract

2 cups fresh blackberries

½ cup all-purpose flour

½ teaspoon ground cinnamon

4 tablespoons salted butter, at room temperature

1. Preheat the oven to 350°F. Grease a 9-inch springform pan.

2. In a large bowl, whisk together the pancake mix, lavender, and ¾ cup of the sugar. Add the melted butter, milk, eggs, and vanilla and stir until just combined. Spoon the batter into the prepared pan. Sprinkle the blackberries over the batter.

3. In a separate small bowl, combine the flour, the remaining ¼ cup of sugar, and the cinnamon. Add the room-temperature butter and mix with your hands until the mixture is moist and a crumble forms. Sprinkle the crumble evenly over the fruit.

4. Bake until the crumble is golden and a toothpick inserted into the center comes out clean, 45 to 55 minutes. Let the buckle cool for 5 minutes. Serve warm or at room temperature. Store any leftovers at room temperature covered for 3 to 4 days.

....

If you don't have any Everyday Pancake Mix prepared, you can combine 1½ cups all-purpose flour with 2 teaspoons baking powder and use in place of the pancake mix.

....

If you're not into lavender, just omit it, or use 1 teaspoon of cardamom in its place. However, if you've never tried lavender, don't be afraid to use it. I love the subtle floral flavor it adds to fruit-based desserts.

FIVE-INGREDIENT
HAZELNUT BROWNIES

MAKES: 9 BROWNIES

PREP TIME: 10 minutes
COOK TIME: 30 minutes
TOTAL TIME: 40 minutes,
plus cooling time

Fun fact: these brownies were kind of the inspiration for this entire cookbook. When I first made them, I couldn't believe they turned out, and that they tasted good, too! Not just good, but really, really good. I figured if I could make such a delicious brownie with just five ingredients, I might be able to pull off a super simple cookbook. Now, I know not all of the recipes here are quite this simple, but what I'm trying to say is that these brownies led the way. Their deliciousness was my inspiration, so I hope you'll give them a try. They're fudgy, super chocolaty with hints of hazelnut throughout, and have a perfectly crinkled top. By using extra-sweet chocolate hazelnut spread, I have eliminated the use of additional sugar . . . and added hints of nutty flavors, too. I've listed the sixth ingredient, chocolate chips, as optional, but, honestly, I would opt in if I were you. They make for an extra-rich brownie that no one can resist.

1 cup chocolate hazelnut spread, such as Nutella

2 large eggs

4 tablespoons salted butter, melted

2 teaspoons pure vanilla extract

½ cup all-purpose flour

½ cup semisweet chocolate chips (optional)

1. Preheat the oven to 350°F. Line an 8 × 8-inch baking dish with parchment paper, leaving a 1-inch overhang on two opposite sides.

2. In a medium bowl, whisk together the hazelnut spread, eggs, butter, and vanilla until smooth, about 1 minute. Add the flour and mix until just combined, 1 to 2 minutes more. Fold in the chocolate chips (if using).

3. Evenly spread the mixture into the prepared baking dish. Bake until the brownies are just set and a tester inserted into the center comes out clean, 25 to 30 minutes.

4. Use the parchment paper overhang to remove the brownies from the pan. Let cool . . . or slice and enjoy warm! Store at room temperature in an airtight container for up to 5 days.

ACKNOWLEDGMENTS

Having an idea for a super simple book is one thing; actually making it into a reality is another. Thank you to my village for all of your support.

An enormous thank-you to everyone at Clarkson Potter for all of the time-consuming back and forth, compromise, and attention to details that were so important to me. To my editor, Amanda Englander, thank you for all of the hours you put into this book. You were as important in getting this book completed as I was. I can't thank you enough for always believing in my vision, responding to my many texts (even into the latest hours of the night), and somehow always knowing exactly what I was trying to say . . . even when what I actually wrote may have made zero sense. You know me and the way I think more than I do sometimes. To Erica Gelbard and Stephanie Davis, thank you for coming up with fun ideas that allowed readers to get to know me. To Stephanie Huntwork and Jen Wang, thank you for your countless hours of work and beautiful details you added to every page of this cookbook. It's gorgeous and you two are to thank for that! To Terry Deal, thank you for reading these pages again and again to catch my mistakes. And to Derek Gullino and Neil Spitkovsky, thank you for your help in producing such a stunning book!

Thank you to the amazing lifestyle photographer Kristen Kilpatrick. You are truly one of the kindest souls I've ever met and I am so thankful to be able to call you a friend. Your photos capture a person beyond where I can see, and you have the ability to make even the most camera-shy person come to life through your lens. Thank you for being a part of the book!

Thank you to my dedicated recipe tester, Grace Rosanova. You put your life on hold to test these recipes, and your comments and suggestions made the book into the much-improved version we have today.

To my very large family of recipe testers, most related in name, and others who became special along the way. Your honest feedback was essential in creating this book, and your company is always highly cherished.

Thank you to my grocery shopper, prop procurer, end-of-day cleaner, prop swapper, goat and chicken handler, and, most important, the best all-around dad a girl could ask for. I couldn't do all that I do without you.

And, finally, to my mom. There aren't enough words to describe how you've helped with this cookbook. From hours of reading and rereading each and every page, to tasting recipes, to late-night phone calls. I could not have done it without you.

INDEX

CLARKSON POTTER is a
trademark and POTTER
with colophon is a registered
trademark of Penguin
Random House LLC.

Library of Congress
Cataloging-in-Publication
Data is available upon
request.

ISBN 978-0-525-57707-2
Ebook 978-0-525-57708-9

Printed in China

Book and cover design by
Jen Wang

Cover photography by
Tieghan Gerard

All interior photographs are
© 2019 by Tieghan Gerard
except: page 3, Michelle
Parker; pages 8, 23, and 134,
Kristen Kilpatrick; and page
251, Amy Batog for
Anthropologie.

11

First Edition